Nation Against State

Nation Against State

A New Approach to Ethnic Conflicts and
the Decline of Sovereignty

GIDON GOTTLIEB

COUNCIL ON FOREIGN RELATIONS PRESS

NEW YORK

COUNCIL ON FOREIGN RELATIONS BOOKS

The Council on Foreign Relations, Inc., is a nonprofit and nonpartisan organization devoted to promoting improved understanding of international affairs through the free exchange of ideas. The Council does not take any position on questions of foreign policy and has no affiliation with, and receives no funding from, the United States government.

From time to time, books and monographs written by members of the Council's research staff or visiting fellows, or commissioned by the Council, or written by an independent author with critical review contributed by a Council study or working group are published with the designation "Council on Foreign Relations Book." Any book or monograph bearing that designation is, in the judgment of the Committee on Studies of the Council's Board of Directors, a responsible treatment of a significant international topic worthy of presentation to the public. All statements of fact and expressions of opinion contained in Council books are, however, the sole responsibility of the author.

If you would like more information on Council publications, please write the Council on Foreign Relations, 58 East 68th Street, New York, NY 10021, or call the Publications Office at (212)734-0400.

Copyright © 1993 by the Council on Foreign Relations®, Inc.
All rights reserved.
Printed in the United States of America.

Library of Congress Cataloging-in-Publication Data

Gottlieb, Gidon
  Nation against state : a new approach to ethnic conflict and the
decline of sovereignty / Gidon Gottlieb
      p. cm.
    Includes index.
    ISBN 0-87609-156-7 : $14.95—ISBN 0-87609-158-3 : $22.95
      1. Europe—History—Autonomy and independence movements.
2. Asia, Central—History—Autonomy and independence movements.
3. Europe—Ethnic relations.   4. Asia, Central—Ethnic relations.
I. Title.
D2009.G68 1993   93-31715
940—dc20   CIP

  94   95   96   EB   10   9   8   7   6   5   4   3   2
Cover Design: Kuan Chang

CONTENTS

PREFACE

This book is the offshoot of a discussion group on the theme of "A Changing World Order," which I directed at the Council on Foreign Relations under the chairmanship of the Hon. Elliot Richardson in 1991. I wish to thank Messrs. Daniel Patrick Moynihan, Henry Kissinger, Thomas Pickering and Virendra Dayal who led the group's discussions. I also wish to express my gratitude to the Arthur Ross Foundation to which this book is properly dedicated, to the Hoover Institution whose assistance made this book possible, to the Ford Foundation, and to Dean Geoffrey Stone, of the Law School of the University of Chicago, for granting a leave of absence during which this work could be done.

I owe a particular debt of gratitude to Nicholas X. Rizopoulos, the Director of Studies of the Council, for his vigorous and incisive editing of the manuscript and to John Temple Swing, the Executive Vice President of the Council, for his unflagging interest and encouragement. I also wish to express my appreciation to David Kellogg for his imaginative interest, to David Haproff and to Judy Train for firmly shepherding this work to publication.

viii   Finally, my special thanks to my dear wife An-
toinette for her patience while I was working on this text
that kept her away from cherished horizons.

The reader will appreciate that it will have been
impossible to go on "updating" sections of the book
dealing with current events in the former Yugoslavia, in
Northern Ireland, Cyprus, Kurdistan, and elsewhere
beyond the point when the manuscript was ready for
publication toward the end of February 1993. I beg his or
her indulgence.

Gidon Gottlieb
New York, April 10, 1993.

INTRODUCTION

A work entitled "Nation Against State" could be expected to address religion, culture, language, and the roots of nationalism. I wish to advise the reader that this book turns in a different direction; it develops instead innovative approaches for contending with brutal conflicts waged in the name of nationhood. The prevailing doctrines of statecraft currently invoked in efforts to check these conflicts evolved in an age when the scourge of war arose between states rather than within them. The basic conflicts that now threaten international peace have little in common with those that arose during the heyday of fascism and communism, when the nation-state reigned supreme. The dominant norms of international law and diplomacy are ill adapted to coping with the kind of strife that has erupted in Yugoslavia and in the Caucasus and that could become common elsewhere in Eurasia.

The United States, the major World powers, and the United Nations need to fashion responses to conflicts in which self determination or the rights of people

x   are at issue.[1] The political and juridical mindsets with which ethnic and national strife have habitually been addressed are not equal to the task. The focus in this book is on the political and juridical concepts that gird this mindset. It is meant to reprogram, to remap the parameters within which these conflicts can be dealt with. From Bosnia to Azerbaijan the stakes for the warring sides are expressed in terms of independence, of statehood, of homeland, of boundaries, of autonomy, and of sovereignty. These notions need to be deconstructed, taken apart and reassembled in a different way for a better fit to the national and ethnic problems that flourish in the post–Cold War world.

   Nation Against State does not aspire to clear a path in the definitional jungle that has blossomed around the issues of nationalism and ethnicity. In regard to culture, religion, language, and the phenomenon of nationalism, the wisest course for a book of this nature is to do no more than point to writings that serve as the modern foundation for work in this field.* In the pages on Ireland, Cyprus, the Kurds, the Azerbaijanis, the Armenians, and on Yugoslavia I have endeavored only to show the potential role and function of new ideas in the search for a settlement. This was done without trying to enrich our knowledge of these societies, although their particular histories and their unique circumstances do require further enquiry and research.

   The term "nation" is mired in difficult disputations. E. H. Hobsbawm has it about right: "Most of this

---

* See the biliographical note on nationalism and ethnicity at the end of this book.

literature [on nationalism] has turned on the question: What is a (or the) nation? For the chief characteristic of this way of classifying groups of human beings is that it is in some ways primary and fundamental for the social existence, or even the individual identification, of its members, no satisfactory criterion can be discovered for deciding which of the many human collectivities should be labelled in this way. . . . How indeed could it be otherwise, given that we are trying to fit historically novel, emerging, changing and, even today, far from universal entities into a framework of permanence and universality? Moreover, the criteria used for this purpose—language, ethnicity or whatever—are themselves fuzzy, shifting and ambiguous and as useless for purposes of the traveller's orientation as cloud-shapes are compared to landmarks."[2] Where objective definitions fail, subjective ones have fared no better, although they are perhaps closer to the mark. Ernest Renan is frequently cited for the proposition that a nation is a daily plebiscite. To cite Hobsbawm again, "As an initial working assumption any suficiently large body of people whose members regard themselves as members of a "nation", will be treated as such. . . . The "nation" as conceived by nationalism, can be recognized prospectively; the real "nation" can only be recognized *a posteriori*."[3] It may be true, as Senator Moynihan alleges, that Hobsbawm's work is directed at denying—against the experience of our time—that the category of nation has proven more powerful than the category of class which was privileged in socialist thought[4]. His insight on the "mollusc-like" nature of the nation is nevertheless a salutary warning to those who would invest too much meaning into an essentially impalpable concept.

The word "ethnic," for its part, is also worn and altered by long usage in an immigration society. By and large it has come to signify that which pertains to kinship, to blood ties, to common origin and descent, although in American parlance it has acquired "an association with foreignness," with foreign languages and cultures.[5]

Having renounced any definitional aspirations, this leaves the question what is meant in *this* book by the terms "nation" and "ethnic group." The answer is somewhat circular. It suffices for our purposes here to say that nations and ethnic groups are those collective entities in which prominent political spokesmen and personalities voice their claims in terms of independence, of self determination, of minority rights, of autonomy, or of secession. Rather than identify these collective entities in subjective, objective, or other terms, they are identified as groups on whose behalf claims of a particular nature are made. Nor need we go into the question whether they have a right to make such claims or examine the grounds on which they are advanced. This meaning should nevertheless exclude groups of a religious character whose claims have features that set them apart from national communities and other ethnic groups.

A third notion—that of a "people"—must also be identified. It features in much of the literature and juridical texts on self determination. It has been widely used during the decolonization period in the grant of independence to former colonial territories of a multi-ethnic, multi-tribal or multi-cultural character. It features also in international agreements on the international protection of human rights, notably in the International Covenants on Civil and Political Rights and on Economic and

Social Rights. These treaties and the resolutions of the United Nations that mention the word "people" have carefully avoided giving it a defined meaning. But, as we shall see, the practice of the international community has been to give that notion a territorial connotation, rather than an ethnic or even a cultural one.

These initial comments are the setting for a book which opens with an outline of concepts specifically adapted to contending with the claims of nations and peoples that have no state of their own.

CHAPTER 1

The Changing System of States

Making room for nations trying to break loose from states that rule over them is a pressing issue for world stability and peace; but so is the avoidance of global fragmentation. Paradoxically, the struggle for the creation of new states is taking place at a time when older states are moving toward broader associations and when the very notion of statehood has lost substance. Both phenomena are aspects of the eroding sovereignty of states: an erosion that reflects the declining utility of borders in an era of missile technology and of the unstoppable flow of ideas and capital. Yet Serbs, Croats, Bosnian Muslims, Armenians, Azerbaijanis, Abkhazians, Georgians, Sikhs, Kurds, and Palestinians are currently consumed by cruel wars to realize national aspirations. These are nations that do not issue directly from the old colonial empires of the West. Their emergence is an aspect of the transformations in the world system as a whole.

A new space for these nations must be found without aggravating disorders in the society of states. The issue is: What kind of space? Must it take the form of conventional statehood? And, as a corollary, what can the international community do about ethnic strife?

1

2   A territorial approach to ethnic conflicts, granting self-rule or statehood in a given area to most of the nations and peoples that want it now, would result in scores of new sovereign states. While the creation of some new states may be necessary or inevitable, the fragmentation of international society into hundreds of independent territorial entities is a recipe for an even more dangerous and anarchic world. Moreover, a territorial approach to the resolution of ethnic conflicts often involves harsh components: the partition of territories, the revision of international and internal borders, the transfer of populations, and the establishment of ethnic homogeneity. It offers "clean" and simple "solutions," but it also seeds new conflicts. In Africa, in Asia, and in Europe, challenges to existing international boundaries to make room for new states could have catastrophic consequences. Past efforts to redraw the map of the world were not particularly successful. The 1919 Versailles peace settlement established borders that did not satisfy the peoples of Europe. The treaties of Sèvres in 1920 and of Lausanne in 1923, which disposed of Ottoman lands, failed to bring peace to their inhabitants.

The tried and tested alternatives to the territorial approach have not shown great promise either. These alternatives are essentially of a juridical character: the international protection of human rights and the creation of special minority rights regimes. In places like Iraq and the Balkans, minority regimes turned out to be nothing more than an elaborate hoax that abandoned minorities to ruthless oppression.[1] The juridical protection of minorities in dictatorships or in states without a genuine democratic tradition is a futile enterprise. Where a state is indifferent to the rights of its inhabitants, it cannot be expected to be careful of the rights of minorities. Complex and sophisticated legal solutions to the minorities problem work only in states with a mature rule of law. Indeed, 75 years after the collapse of the Russian, Ottoman, and Austro-Hungarian empires, the ethnic problems that are their legacy remain unsolved. In the crude political environment of popular hatreds, of one-man, one-party (or military) rulers, more is needed for real protection than paper barriers. Neither the United Nations nor the United States can credibly address ethnic strife merely in terms of proposals for the protection of human rights or constitutional guarantees.

The deficiencies of the territorial and of the juridical approaches are painfully apparent. Western statecraft and the UN community require a wider set of approaches for dealing with national and ethnic conflicts.

In this book, I outline a third approach for addressing ethnic conflicts, "states plus nations." This strategy is meant to offer alternatives that proponents both of the territorial (statehood) and of the juridical (minority and human rights) solutions neglect. It is rendered possible by changing attitudes to the sovereignty of states.

The states-plus-nations approach involves sets of related concepts:

- *Status*—the extension of the international system of states to make room also for a system of nations. This can occur through the gradual opening of international organizations, as well as the granting of a new international status to participating new nations (as distinct from states), albeit in a manner that does not require the creation of new territorial states.

- *Competence*—the deconstruction of the sovereignty of states and the redistribution of some of its attributes to different hands. The way to accomplish this is through the allocation of jurisdictional, functional, and territorial competence along new principles.

- *Borders*—the delimitation of a variety of boundary lines and functional borders for different purposes, such as for security arrangements. This approach borrows, for populated territories, practices that are analogous to those of urban zoning.

- *National home distinct from state*—the recognition of the notion of a "national home" (*patrie* or *heimat*), which is embedded in the consciousness of many nations. A national home is an entity with defined geographic limits that can, but often do not, correspond to state boundaries. It is an entity that exists over, and sometimes beyond, state limits: a national-home regime would stipulate the national rights to be enjoyed in the national home without prejudice to the integrity of the states involved. It would constitute an overlay, so to speak, over an existing state.

- *Citizenship*—the adoption of different layers of personal status expressing the links between the individual and the state, as well as those between the individual and his nation. These can be embodied in a distinction between "citizenship," derived from the state, and "nationality," derived from the nation.

- *Forms of association*—the creation of new kinds of attachments or union among nations and peoples on the one hand, and between nations and states on the other. This can occur through the establishment of functional associations of peoples side by side with associations of states.

The political will to find negotiated solutions remains a precondition to the peaceful resolution of ethnic conflicts. The cultivation of a commitment to negotiate requires the wise application of political and economic leverage by the great powers. It requires also a vision of the future that reconciles the claims of different sides; that vision must be one they can prefer over the struggle in which they are engaged.

Other dimensions of the traditional state system are also undergoing rapid change. The economic and political integration of the American-Japanese-European triad and the readiness of the international community to intervene in countries like Somalia and Haiti, in circumstances that until recently were beyond its competence, point to a shift in the character of the sovereignty of states.

This study is organized around three levels of issues: the decline of sovereignty, ethnic conflicts, and collective intervention and collective security. Throughout, the emphasis remains on the larger issue of ethnic conflicts.[2]

CHAPTER 2

Sovereignty Diminished

This much is now clear: the American victory in the Cold War has transformed the international order. Its resonance is magnified by the collapse of the Soviet Union, by the emergence of Russia and the other states of the would-be Commonwealth of Independent States (CIS), and by the feverish reordering of relations among the states of Europe. Continental powers break up, and others take shape; from Maastricht to Minsk, the features of the world we knew have been modified beyond recognition.

But do these events intimate an even more profound change, a change in the system of international relations itself, or do they merely signal the defeat of an empire and the ascendancy of other powers? In fact, what we see is a mutation in the character of the state system, as well as the passing of an empire.

We are witnessing the end of a phase of history in which ideologies of the right and of the left idealized the state as the preferred instrument of progress. Communists and fascists expected the state to be the vehicle of economic growth, of modernity, and of social justice. The failure of these ideologies and the inability of governments to provide what was expected of them coincided with the failure of the market to remedy social inequities.[1] It has led to more sober expectations about what the governments of even the most powerful nations can and will do.

A stable international order is *not* now within reach. The two previously tried roads to international stability—domination and equilibrium—are equally beyond us. What is in place now is a form of benign and largely ineffective international supervision. This "managed disorder" is loosely directed by the Group of 7 (G-7) in the economic arena and by the United States—within the Security Council and the North Atlantic Treaty Organization (NATO)—in military matters. The limits of this management became apparent in 1992, when Europe and the UN allowed the civil war in Yugoslavia to run its course without forcing it to a halt, and when the G-7 failed to agree on steps that would halt the decline of the economies of Europe.

Two other fundamental processes are unfolding at the same time: the accelerating integration of the states of Europe (albeit in the face of rising domestic popular opposition) and uncertain efforts to safeguard a nonadversarial mode of relations in the American-Japanese-European triad. In the meantime, Russia and Ukraine are undergoing the great mutation from communism toward the market system that will move them in a direction that is still unknown to them and to the rest of the world, while an awesome nuclear arsenal remains in their uncertain hands.

In the event, an agenda of hard questions involving the nature of sovereignty in the international system must be addressed:

Nations. Is it necessary to complement the state system with a new space for nations? Is it possible to find

8 nonterritorial solutions for some of the peoples striving for self-determination and independence? Can this be done without undermining the stability and integrity of existing states? Is it possible to recognize national rights beyond state limits without jeopardizing the territorial integrity of states?

Intervention. Is it necessary to legitimize collective intervention into the domestic realm of states to support a new agenda of urgent concerns? Are ethnic groups subjected to genocidal attacks entitled to international protection? Is intervention warranted to prevent the spread of weapons of mass destruction, for humanitarian assistance to civilian populations, and in environmental emergencies? Which are the agencies and organizations that should have the power to authorize such intervention?

Economic and Political Communities. Will the preservation of a liberal international economic order require the gradual political integration of the American-Japanese-European triad? Will the United States have to choose between competition and confrontation with its economic rivals, on the one hand, and closer political integration with them, on the other? Can a liberal trade system survive without a commensurate degree of political integration? Indeed, what is the relationship between economic and political integration? How far can political integration be pressed among states divided by history and by culture?

A broad consensus has, in fact, emerged in the United States on much of the agenda for the world order to come. It is not confined to questions of military security and includes the whole range of issues that distinguished Americans such as Cyrus Vance, Elliot Richardson, Theodore Sorensen, Henry Kissinger, Paul Nitze, and others have canvassed in speeches and articles. It is by now the conventional wisdom that curbing population growth, environmental degradation, and weapons of mass destruction; fostering democracy and human rights; and strengthening international institutions must form part of any new world order. Moreover, the international community cannot countenance violent conflicts on the scale of the ongoing Yugoslavian wars if it is to retain credibility as a keeper of the peace. This agenda is supplemented by measures designed to help the states of the former Soviet Union join the community of prosperous, free democratic societies of the West, and to assist other developing countries on a similar path. Yet the success of such steps remains very much in doubt. The American people do not now appear ready to back this agenda with commensurate means and resources.

The new world system is taking shape as a collage of patterns of ordering. Some elements are based on equilibrium, and others on the dominant military position of the United States; still others are based on doctrines of collective security. This world system is not self-correcting, and mistakes will be made. But improvements remain possible.

THE VIEW FROM THE PAST

In 1951 the policy planning staff of the State Department outlined the war aims of the United States in the case of a possible conflict with the Soviet Union. It drew

10   a picture of the world environment that the United States would like to see at the conclusion of a war that would eliminate—or radically modify—the Soviet regime. This effort led to a little-known but important National Security Council document (NSC 79).[2] After the outbreak of the Korean War, the U.S. government was deeply concerned that the conflict might widen into a global war. The Joint Chiefs of Staff requested that the NSC outline clear-cut objectives to serve as a basis for military planning directed toward the winning of the ultimate peace, as well as to the winning of the war. Paul Nitze, who then headed the policy planning staff, assigned the task to Louis Halle, who drafted a paper that met with an enthusiastic response from Dean Acheson: "It is too bad it can't be published; it is the only paper that I have ever seen which might make an impact on the world as great as Keynes's 'The Economic Consequences of the Peace.'"[3] Acheson feared that the subject matter, the analysis, and the recommendations would be misunderstood and criticized. He ordered all copies but one to be destroyed.

      Halle's work and NSC 79 are an ideal starting point for any discussion of the international system after the Cold War. The United States now faces questions about aims in the post–Cold War era similar to those that Nitze's able staff explored with visionary insight forty years ago.

      Another helpful starting point, albeit one much closer to us in time, is the American Assembly's 1991 report *Rethinking America's Security*.[4] It considers how the United States should reorient its relations toward other countries at the end of the Cold War (and in the wake of the Gulf War). These two documents, so different in their nature and intended audience, vividly sketch the direction of American thinking at two defining moments in recent history: the first, when America seriously contemplated war with the Soviets; the second, when the Cold War was won.

The NSC study held that there were four main conceptual alternatives for the construction of a world order in the 1950s:

- Re-creation of the balance of power

- Pax Americana

- Development of alliance systems

- World government

The question worth asking today is whether these alternatives are still meaningful, whether a blend among them is possible, whether they are compatible, and how they can be managed. Of course, these alternatives look different from the vantage point of 1993. The balance of power is a weaker guard—in an increasingly anarchic world—against threats to the peace that often come from domestic disorders. It is also losing salience in an international society in which individual governments have lost much control over civil society and the private economy. The widening commerce in, and availability of, weapons of mass destruction has altered the potential weight of small states that might have access to them. Changes within the great nations of the world are largely immune to the influence of outside powers. The rising velocity in the circulation of capital, people, ideas, and cultures increasingly blurs the dividing line between international affairs and domestic policy. The leading international actors of the recent past are hardly recognizable: Germany, Japan, and Europe are trans-

12 formed; the Soviet Union no longer exists; China is gestating a radical transformation whose nature no one can predict. Now, as then, disorder and anarchy will prevail if no power stands ready to shoulder the burdens of international order.

The "unipolar" moment, in which America's military ascendancy is unchallenged, is not a sufficient basis for a Pax Americana in a world in which economic issues are now paramount. It is hard to disagree with the authors of NSC 79, who asserted that a Pax Americana ran contrary to the American ethos, and that a policy based upon this doctrine would cause worldwide hostility and resistance to the United States. Indeed, few would disagree that a Pax Americana is beyond the means of the United States to impose and contrary to the will of the American people at a time when the country ardently wishes to put its own house in order. Pax Americana is no more of an alternative today than it was in 1950. The rush of nations previously subjugated by communist rulers to share the joys and prosperity of consumerism is neither a plebiscite for Pax Americana nor an acquiescence to American hegemony. The triumph of market economics and of liberal democracy is not synonymous with unchallenged American supremacy. Moreover, there are no signs that the United States is developing the desire, let alone the determination or the means, to bear the responsibilities of world leadership. The deep cuts in the armed forces, every opinion poll, and every economic analysis point in the opposite direction.

While a Pax Americana was not and is not a serious alternative for a stable international system, American elites continue to think in global terms—in what amounts to a "Via Americana," or "American Way."

More modestly, thinkers in other nations are preoccupied with regional concerns and with the relations of their countries to other powers. The design of "global" visions is an American specialty. It has features that connote a mind-set that differs from that which prevails elsewhere. This mind-set stresses single-issue "policies" over the rich range of interests that characterize relations with foreign countries; "processes" and "institutions" over substance, over strategic objectives, and over the identification of nations as allies to build on; "international law" over particular local histories and regional contexts; "grand designs" and "universal" arrangements over local ones; the general over the particular; geographic "areas" over individual countries. It is a mind-set that glosses over particularisms and strives for broad solutions. It is truly idiosyncratic, in that it is not very common among the elites of other lands.

There is a disjunction between America's reluctance to impose its ways on other nations and the American eagerness to tell the world how it should be shaped and ordered. Blueprints made in the enlightened, rich nations—the G-7, for example—are advanced with little concern for the views and positions of the more populous, poverty-stricken, and less-efficient countries. With the best of intentions, this mind-set wounds and slights those who have not anointed the world order architects with either authority or legitimacy. The better world order designs will have to be negotiated with the "consumers" of these designs. A unilaterally proclaimed new world order has the potential to promote resistance and to arouse resentments that could well defeat its purpose. It is striking how rapidly this concept fell into disuse; it even disappeared from the Republican party platform for the 1992 elections.

14   This mind-set reflects the centrality of law and of constitutionalism in the American polity, a phenomenon long familiar to observers of the American scene. It is evident in a profound commitment to the rule of law in international relations—a commitment that foreign elites do not seriously entertain. But attitudes may change abroad before they change in America as community law takes root in Europe and, in the future, perhaps also the CIS.

THE DECLINE OF SOVEREIGNTY

The twin notions of state and sovereignty—and their two corollaries, the notions of consent and treaties—dominate the conceptual setting of diplomatic relations. These notions are the anchor for discourse on changes in the international system: all changes, it is said, must flow from the consent of states—that is to say, the consent of their rulers.

      Sovereignty has meant different things at different times.[5] The history of this concept is the history of Western political thought. In 1921, in a lengthy scholarly essay, Secretary of State Robert Lansing identified two major elements of sovereignty: the power to compel obedience to the sovereign will and the possession of physical force superior to any other that makes such compulsion possible. He did not speak of a *right* to compel, but of a *power* to compel. In his view, the territorial component of sovereignty was not essential, but the state as an organized community of individuals was of importance. Sovereignty, he argued, is a political concept, it pertains to power over people, it is a power to be exercised over persons rather than over territory.[6]

But Lansing's analysis failed to do justice to the territorial component of sovereignty. The right to exclusive control over territory has long been a central ingredient of the sovereignty of states. Indeed, much of international law governing the jurisdiction of states is premised upon it. Moreover, the existence of a territory under government control is one of the juridical criteria of statehood. The distinction between *power over people* and *power over territory* is a useful one to make, for it singles out two aspects of sovereignty that are best addressed separately: disputes involving the right of peoples to self-determination and territorial disputes among them.

Writing in 1990, former Secretary of State George Shultz returned to the topic that had so preoccupied his predecessor.[7] He pointed out that today, the meaning of borders is changing, and so is the notion of sovereignty. The irrepressible movement of ideas, people, and goods requires leaders to be politically flexible and economically sophisticated. In today's world, he argued, people will have a right to define themselves but not to wall themselves off. Constructs based on absolute sovereignty and on rigid borders cannot provide the vision for settling difficult problems of self-determination.

In time of all-out war, the sovereignty of states occupies center stage, just as their armed forces dominate the international scene. Nevertheless, the notion of the sovereignty of states remains under assault. A synthesis of the elements leading to its erosion includes both normative and objective factors. This erosion is occurring on a number of planes. In Europe the redistribution of attributes of sovereignty is taking place at different levels, at the supranational level of the European Community (EC) and at the level of infranational regional authorities. At the same time, profound normative

16   changes in regard to individual rights and social stan-
       dards have shrunk the perimeter of the exclusive juris-
       diction of the Twelve. The Helsinki Final Act, the
       Charter of Paris, and the practices of the Conference on
       Security and Cooperation in Europe (CSCE) have rein-
       forced the pattern of international scrutiny in human
       rights matters and in the treatment of minorities.

       In the EC the distribution of sovereign authority
       between Brussels, the national governments, and their
       domestic subdivisions remains unsettled. The formerly
       exclusive right of states to make laws, raise taxes, and
       administer justice is now widely shared with the Euro-
       pean institutions. Following the Danish voters' rejection
       of the Maastricht treaty on European union, greater
       emphasis has gone to the principle of "subsidiarity,"
       which requires that the Community and its institutions
       stay clear of decisions that are better taken at the local
       level and at the level of member states. In 1992 the near
       defeat by French voters of the Maastricht treaty (it was
       approved by the slenderest of margins) and continued
       popular wariness about European integration, reflected
       in the Swiss rejection of the European Economic Space,
       pointed to real trouble for the architects of European
       union. The swing of the pendulum away from national
       sovereignty and toward the supranational institutions in
       Brussels may already have peaked.

       The European Community created different jurid-
       ical spaces to erase internal sovereign frontiers for the
       movement of goods, of capital, and (since the Schengen
       agreement) also for the free movement of persons. At
       the local level, the establishment of regions astride
       national frontiers signals the emergence of new tiers of
       authorities that do not coincide with those of tradi-
       tional states. For example, Savoy and the Leman now

form one region for certain defined purposes (although one shore of the lake is within the Community, while the other remains outside); the Trieste region brings together the authorities of the historic Trieste hinterland (neutral Austria plus, presumably, Slovenia to replace Yugoslavia).[8]

The erosion of state sovereignty has sparked a backlash in which traditional nationalist elements have combined with economic interests who fear that the removal of protective barriers will hurt their position and privileges. In France it has led to a split among the parties of the right. In Britain it has revived unease among Tory members of Parliament, as well as calls for the application of the principle of subsidiarity domestically to Scotland. In Germany, in mid-June 1992 the federal government and the sixteen federal landers were virtually deadlocked in their efforts to change the constitution so as to adapt it to the Maastricht blueprint. The principle of subsidiarity is invoked not only between Brussels and the member states, but also between the German federal government and its component landers. Two issues involving this principle, which affect the federal character of Germany, remained to be resolved: the extent to which the landers will have an effective veto on any future transfer of sovereignty to the Community, and the extent to which they will have "co–decision-making" rights with the federal government in the making of EC legislation.

Even beyond the Community, where the erosion of sovereignty is most apparent, the readiness to intervene in situations that until recently were exclusively within the domestic jurisdiction of states is apparent. The examples are striking; the fact that they involve mostly developments taking place with the formal con-

18   sent of governments does not detract from their significance. What matters is the extent of the departure from traditional practices: The arms control agreements between the United States and the former Soviet Union establish intrusive on-site inspection regimes that would have been unthinkable until recently. The UN took an active role in monitoring national elections in Nicaragua and in Namibia that, in earlier times, would have been considered an intervention in domestic affairs. In 1992 the United States and other members of the Organization of American States (OAS) considered the dispatch of an international peacekeeping force to Haiti to reestablish order and to help restore democratic rule. The International Monetary Fund and the countries of the Club of Paris attach conditionality clauses to financial help bearing on the domestic economic and fiscal policies of borrowers. Aid is tied to economic reforms establishing market economies. In the United States, the Congress is challenging most-favored-nation status for countries that violate human rights standards. Increasingly, the United States and the states of Europe assert jurisdiction beyond national territorial limits to govern activities taking place elsewhere. The United States exercises extraterritorial jurisdiction for a number of purposes: to govern activities on the seabed of the continental shelf, to enforce Securities and Exchange Commission regulations and antitrust legislation, for drug interdiction, and for the war on terror.

Moreover, some voices suggest that the international community should intervene to prevent the spread of nuclear weapons in violation of nonproliferation treaty obligations. In the view of others, environmental emergencies—such as the operation of unsafe nuclear reactors—may warrant forcible intervention to protect states from another Chernobyl.

Taken together, these developments, trends, norms, and institutional changes signify a steady encroachment into the domain of state sovereignty, which has been a defining element of the international order since the seventeenth century. But it is important not to overstate the point. The sovereignty of states remains a doctrine with wide appeal, perhaps nowhere more so than in the UN and among authoritarian states in the developing world. The latter see in the legal requirement of strict respect for sovereign rights a useful doctrinal shield against international involvement in their domestic practices. State sovereignty is a doctrine that continues to elicit frequent verbal support even as international practice moves steadily away from it. The UN and the other interstate organizations must continue to invoke it.

The erosion of state sovereignty is taking place at a time when the creation of new states has been so common that it is increasingly difficult to counter demands for the establishment of yet other states, especially when the demands are pressed by peoples with a high international profile. Different trends have combined to debase the coinage of statehood: many states that do not "deserve" to be states have been created in the past few years. The emergence of states like Slovakia, the collapse of other states, like Somalia, and the continued existence of insignificant ministates confirm that statehood is no longer a "big deal." In this setting, the denial of statehood to the peoples who have engaged in a long and painful struggle or who continue to resist alien rule is increasingly difficult to justify even as the imperative

20   of limiting the number of new states is becoming more
pressing.

Legitimacy and Sovereignty

The structure of international society is based on consent. But the notion of consent has tended to remain
narrow and legalistic. It has generally meant the consent
of recognized governments in power, to the exclusion of
other parties. It has typically left out other vigorous and
turbulent actors on the international scene, such as national and ethnic groups and minorities. Only in 1991,
in a resolution on humanitarian assistance to the victims
of armed conflicts, did the UN General Assembly refer
to the consent of parties and countries, and not just of
states.

International legal discourse has been thrown into
disarray by the intensifying erosion of sovereignty. The
international legal system of the modern age still reflects
the concepts and structures of times when the doctrine
of the sovereign equality of states more closely tracked
their practices. This conceptual setting colors and per-
vades all efforts to address global problems.

The emergence of an international consensus on
what constitutes legitimate rule has a direct bearing on
foreign intervention. Fewer restraints face intervention
in the internal affairs of countries ruled by illegitimate
regimes. The international community has come to an
agreement that only democratic regimes are legitimate.
In its final year, the Soviet Union joined in the re-
markable 1990 document of the Copenhagen meeting of
the Conference on Security and Cooperation in Europe
that stated that "the will of the people, freely and
fairly expressed through periodic and genuine elections,
is the basis of the authority and the legitimacy of all

government."[9] This principle received detailed coverage in the document and was spelled out further in the 1991 Charter of Paris, adopted at the summit meeting of the CSCE states.

International law cannot remain immune to changes in political doctrine. In 1993, for the first time since the 1815 Congress of Vienna, the world is united in its view on what constitutes legitimate rule. This, in itself, is a momentous political development. Liberal democracy is the unchallenged standard of legitimacy almost everywhere on earth. China, North Korea, Cuba, and the fundamentalist Islamic states are alone in advocating other standards. Francis Fukuyama has observed that "as mankind approaches the end of the millennium, the twin crises of authoritarianism and socialist central planning have left only one competitor standing in the ring as an ideology of potentially universal validity: liberal democracy, the doctrine of individual freedom and popular sovereignty."[10]

The full implications of the near global consensus on political legitimacy have not as yet been digested. This consensus will inevitably help erode formal state sovereignty. It must be seen in context, for the international system has not stood still. In the seventeenth century the international order governed relations between European ruling princes, kings, and the pope. Later, the international legal system became one between the rulers and governments of sovereign states. Michael Reisman, a Yale legal scholar whose views are strongly contested, has argued for some time that peoples, and not their rulers, are the true bearers of sovereignty. The new consensus on legitimate rule should reinforce his position. It tends to shift the locus of sovereignty from states (in practice, their rulers) to peoples.

22   The choice between attributing ultimate legal authority to the ruler or to the ruled has been made, and international law theory will have to come to terms with it. The alignment of international law doctrines with the new consensus on legitimate rule will not take place overnight. Many governments, and their judicial servants, will likely resist in order to preserve long-standing privileges and immunities.

It is still widely held that to question the legitimacy of tyrannical regimes, most of which are found in the developing world, can be profoundly dangerous and destabilizing. Thus, the American Assembly has concluded, "Only in extreme cases of emergency or humanitarian need will it be right to set aside the sovereignty of other states."[11]

The emergence of an international consensus on legitimate rule and on the content of human rights augurs the dawn of major changes in international law. This new consensus has the effect of lifting the "corporate veil" of states. It warrants international intervention in the affairs of regimes whose legitimacy and human rights record are grossly unsatisfactory. Deviation from these standards is no longer ignored. Modern international law need no longer insulate rulers like Marcos, Amin, Duvalier, Saddam, Asad, Qaddafi, Noriega, Mobutu, and Castro from international challenges to their right to rule. Once the shift of sovereignty from rulers to their peoples is the accepted norm, the rights of sovereignty should not be theirs to invoke. The maintenance of a regime in power need of itself provide neither immunity nor privileges to tyrants in office. The classical, statist, international order threw a mantle of legitimacy and respectability on rogue regimes that were without a rightful claim to rule in their own countries.

The representation of these rulers in the UN long helped cloak narrow regime interests as those of the hapless people over which they have absolute power. It tended, moreover, to discredit the agencies in which these regimes were seated: Saddam Hussein's Iraq, for example, has long tarnished the UN Commission on Human Rights.

Another notion that may justify the interest of the international community in the protection and defense of democratic regimes (but that remains to be tested) is that democracies do not go to war with each other.[12] The challenge to statist doctrines is not an invitation to global meddling or to intervention by the powerful states of the G-7 into the affairs of the less-fortunate. It is, rather, a plea for recognition that an international system that grants equal privileges and immunities to democratic governments and to the brutal rulers of defenseless populations enjoys little support outside official circles.

The contemporary triumph of the democratic ideal requires some words of caution. Democratic rule may be a necessary but not a sufficient condition for the respect of human rights. The authors of the American Bill of Rights fully recognized that the rights of minorities and of individuals require protection from democratically elected governments. Historian Jacob Talmon brilliantly exposed the danger of the totalitarian tradition in theories of the popular will and in some of the democratic doctrines associated with the French Revolution.[13] In many places democratic electoral practices are designed to inhibit the alternance of governments. In others, like South Africa and Iran, they are restricted to a racial or religious community. In some societies, popular majorities favor the prosecution of holy wars or

24 ethnic wars. Free elections can be the carriers of tyran-
nies: Adolf Hitler was carried into office by a popular
vote. In many states, neither economic and social conditions nor cultural traditions provide a receptive terrain
for democratic practices. But none of these considerations militate in favor of the retention of sovereignty
doctrines that serve as a shield for abuses committed by
tyrannical rulers.

STATES PLUS NATIONS

The fact that scores of nations are struggling for self-
determination calls for fresh thinking about the relationship between states and nations. This question, which
raises the larger question of nationalism, has been sadly
neglected since the Versailles peace settlement. It has
acquired new salience with the dissolution of the Soviet
empire. The issue is whether the time has come to
complement the system of states with a new system of
nations, with legal regimes capable of responding to the
claims of the hundreds of peoples that still aspire to
independence; and whether this can occur without
threatening the integrity of existing states. In other
words, should the system of states be *supplemented
with*—not *replaced by*—a system of nations?

Historians date the "modern" international system
of sovereign and juridically equal territorial states back
to the 1648 Treaty of Westphalia. That system privileged territorial rulers and paid scant attention to the
ethnic and religious affiliations of their peoples. Westphalia was concluded at a time when the aspirations of
subject peoples were of little concern. It was still far too
early to speak of national identities. The awakening and

elevation of the peoples of Europe to the stage of history, where they joined the aristocratic and clerical classes, had to await the French Revolution and unfolded in the nineteenth century. After the First World War, when the map of Europe was made over, the aspirations of the peoples of central Europe and of the Balkans did not dominate the calculations of statesmen, whose primary concern remained the balance of power. The Versailles peace settlement stitched together new countries that bundled into a single state peoples long animated by deep mutual antagonism (for example, the Serbs and Croats in Yugoslavia or the Czechs and Slovaks in Czechoslovakia). The largely rural population of these new countries was kept "in its place" by authoritarian rulers, royal houses, a strong clergy, and small middle classes with their teachers and intellectuals. In the aftermath of the Second World War, these peoples found themselves subjected to the iron fist of communist regimes. In the case of Yugoslavia, the death of Tito and the sudden disintegration of the Soviet empire led to the no less sudden reemergence of the question of nationalities.

To investigate what lies behind the current resurgence of self-determination is to reopen an ancient line of inquiry about the causes of nationalism. The spread of democratic rule and the disintegration of the repressive Soviet empire are no doubt a factor. Also, the difficult economic circumstances in which the newly liberated peoples of Eastern Europe find themselves probably lead many to believe that they can do better under independence. According to a widespread crude belief, national and ethnic feelings will dissipate once democracy and the prosperity of the market reach those peoples. Isaiah Berlin's perceptive essay on nationalism,

26 written in the dark days of the Cold War, is a healthy rejoinder to those who hold that nationalism can be "cured" with the drug of economic growth and with political reform.[14] The disparate stories of different peoples at different times—the Risorgimento, the peoples of Quebec, the Basques, the Scots, the Jurassiens— cannot be understood merely in terms of a reaction to authoritarianism and economic deprivation. The failure of the collectivist ideologies of the right and of the left restored nationalism and religion as the principal providers of "just causes" in societies in which individualism has not displaced the need for group identification. Possibly the passions exhibited at soccer matches and rock music festivals stem from the same craving for collective fervor.

Self-determination unleashed and unchecked by balancing principles constitutes a menace to the society of states. There is simply no way in which all the hundreds of peoples who aspire to sovereign independence can be granted a state of their own without loosening fearful anarchy and disorder on a planetary scale. The proliferation of territorial entities poses exponentially greater problems for the control of weapons of mass destruction and multiplies situations in which external intervention could threaten the peace. It increases problems for the management of all global issues, including terrorism, AIDS, the environment, and population growth. It creates conditions in which domestic strife in remote territories can drag powerful neighbors into local hostilities, creating ever widening circles of conflict. Events in the aftermath of the breakup of the Soviet Union drove this point home. Like Russian dolls, ever smaller ethnic groups dwelling in larger units emerged to secede and to demand independence. Georgia, for

example, has to contend with the claims of South Osse-
tians and Abkhazians for independence, just as the Russian Federation is confronted with the separatism of
Tartaristan. An international system made up of several
hundred independent territorial states cannot be the
basis for global security and prosperity.

A 1992 study published by the Carnegie Endowment for International Peace attempted to evaluate self-
determination movements from a perspective that considers both their legitimacy and their strength, as well as
the desirability of safeguarding existing states.[15] This
was offered as a guide for U.S. policy on whether or not
to become involved, and to what end. It described the
options in classical terms: "In evaluating self-determination movements, the U.S. government and the world
community generally will reach a crossroads at which
they must decide to remain neutral, support the preservation of an existing state within its current borders, or
back the creation of a new independent state."[16] The
states-plus-nations approach is meant to expand the
range of options so concisely outlined in the Carnegie
study.

The current vogue of self-determination has tended
to obscure the doctrines that place restraints on its exercise. It is widely understood to lead of necessity to
independent statehood (although international practice
does not invariably confirm this). This principle is
hemmed in by important balancing doctrines: by norms
of international law relating to the territorial integrity of
states and the inviolability of borders: by doctrines governing the prohibition of intervention in internal affairs,
and the protection of human rights and minorities. The
balance between these principles is clearly expressed in
the UN Declaration on the Principles of International

28   Law Governing Peaceful Coexistence and Friendly Relations among States.[17] The prohibition of the premature recognition of states and the absence of a right to secede are germane to the management of self-determination issues.

In the present passionate climate, it often will not do merely to restrain the claim of self-determination. A credible and substantial outlet must be found for the aspirations of nations chafing under "foreign" rule or restive in a setting of territorial promiscuity. It is not possible to stem the flood of demands for self-determination by discriminating between "worthy" claims and those that are not, and to do so on the basis of the democratic and humane character of the claimants. The legitimacy and vitality of the claims of peoples to a state of their own turn on considerations of a much richer texture. They flow from history, from wrongs suffered, from sacrifices made, and from symbolic and mythical elements that move nations in ways that transcend cold considerations of statecraft. Nations caught up in such struggles pay scant attention to the opinions of outsiders. No simple set of criteria can identify the "meritorious" claimants to statehood. A broader approach is necessary to do them justice. Guidelines such as those Secretary of State James Baker enunciated in 1991[18] and those the EC adopted that same year (the Badinter principles)[19] for the recognition of new states in Eastern Europe were an attempt to orchestrate a collective response to fast-moving events. As the tragic war in Bosnia demonstrates, however, it is idle to expect that peoples animated by ancient fears and archaic hatreds will be much influenced by the norms developed in the chancelleries of Paris, London, and Bonn. Nations and peoples in the throes of struggles with hated neighbors want a place of their own both at home and in international society. The issue that the United States and the rest of the world must face is whether this place can be found only through the creation of additional *territorial* states or whether other forms of nationhood, sometimes of a nonterritorial character, can be established alongside the traditional states of the international system.

The international system has but two principal methods for addressing national and ethnic claims. It can address them either within state boundaries or through the creation of new states. Minority treaties dominated state practice in the years that followed the First World War. Under the then prevailing standards, a state's treatment of its own nationals was not a proper subject for international concern in the absence of a treaty to the contrary. The Allies designed the minority treaties as part of the settlement of the First World War.[20] The treaties were imposed on the new states in the domains of the former Austro-Hungarian empire. Provisions governing the rights of minorities were also introduced in the treaties of Sèvres and of Lausanne. National feelings were a fervent force at the Paris peace conference.[21] Woodrow Wilson believed that nothing was more likely to disturb the peace than the treatment that might in certain circumstances be meted out to minorities. But the cold logic of the balance of power prevailed, and geopolitical considerations received priority over the claims of small nations for independence. The synthetic states of Yugoslavia and of Czechoslovakia were created without much regard for the aspirations of the nations that were forced into them. The borders of Hungary were drawn in a manner that left nearly a third of the Hungarian nation of 15 million outside the limits of the Hungarian state. The issue of

30   the treatment of Hungarian minorities in Romania, Slovakia, and Serbia, and of the rights of the Hungarian state to come to their defense, has the potential of a crisis no less grave than the one that has ravaged Yugoslavia.

The mechanism for the safeguard of minority rights was cumbersome and difficult, involving contrived procedures in the Council of the League of Nations. Minorities not covered by treaty were left, diplomatically and juridically, to the mercy of their own governments. On the whole, the minority regimes failed to protect the security, culture, autonomy, dignity, and prosperity of small nations like the Kurds that did not achieve their independence. The international law principle forbidding intervention in the domestic affairs of states retained its full vitality and received priority over the protection of individuals and ethnic groups.

The interwar minority treaties were superseded after the Second World War by the gradual development of international human rights standards that established norms for the treatment by a state of *all* persons within its boundaries, and not merely for its minorities. Minority regimes were resented by states singled out for international scrutiny.[22] No such objection could be made to universal human rights standards that applied to all. These are intended to govern the treatment of all persons everywhere, including the treatment by a state of its own citizens. They removed, for example, the diplomatic impediment that inhibited the Vatican from protesting the Reich's treatment of its Jewish subjects.

At the close of the Second World War, the United Nations Organization was established with the aspiration to correct the deficiencies of the League system. The UN Charter abandoned the League system for the protection of minorities.[23] The League scheme for the protection of minority rights was discarded in favor of the new commitment to the preservation of human rights. The international protection of human rights focused on the rights of individuals, rather than on the rights of communities and peoples. Minority rights were no longer addressed as such. They fell into neglect as the banner of human rights was raised ever higher. But even as the international law on human rights developed, the remedies for their protection remained woefully inadequate. Until very recently, the voting majority in the UN was made up of authoritarian states, if not worse. This majority persistently resisted efforts to seriously monitor and enforce their implementation. However, the 1948 Universal Declaration on Human Rights and the 1966 Covenants on Civil, Political, Economic and Social Rights gradually led to the principle that the violation of human rights is a matter of international concern. The 1975 Helsinki Final Act secured the formal adherence to these norms by the states of the communist bloc.

The reemergence of nationalism that we are witnessing in the former realms of the czars, of the Habsburgs, and of the Ottomans takes place in the context of failed minority regimes, an emphasis on the rights of individuals, and a neglect of the rights of nations within states (other than their right to self-determination). The juridical-diplomatic context for the struggles of newly liberated nations drives them relentlessly toward independence.

The sharp divide between the status of a territorial state and that of a national minority inflames passions for independence. The international order has no halfway houses in matters of status. Yet the creation of

32   richer, more varied forms of national existence remains possible. Halfway houses can be established between territorial independence and autonomy. These may satisfy the needs of some nations, like the Iraqi Kurds, that find the road to full independence barred by powerful neighbors and by geopolitical concerns of the great powers. Admittedly, peoples struggling for self-determination will often not be satisfied with anything less than full territorial independence. For such peoples, halfway houses are halfway stations on the road to statehood; they are by their very nature impermanent solutions.

In the international system statehood is a juridical status, with defined rights, privileges, duties, and immunities. All derogations and modifications must be negotiated and settled by agreement. With regard to statehood, there is no move yet—to borrow a phrase from the eminent legal historian Sir Henry Maine—from status to contract. The divide between the status of statehood and all other forms of political organization has contributed to the elevation of the value of independence beyond what it might otherwise have been. The many types of quasi-states, associated states, federal states, and state communities designed by modern statecraft have by and large not been responsive to the demands of nations that are still struggling to break free. Many strive not only to rule themselves but also to achieve a fuller access to the benefits and entitlements of international life.

Gorbachev's Union Treaty

In 1991 Mikhail Gorbachev made an interesting attempt to devise a solution to the nationalities problem. He attempted to find a way of reconciling the unity of the

USSR with the separatism of its republics. The Soviet Union was in its death throes. The reasons why this effort failed need not detain us here; they have much to do with the collapse of communism as a system of government and with the rapid disintegration of the Soviet economy. The proposed, but aborted, Union treaty remains of interest because it outlined a bold compromise between the unity of the state and the independence of its members.[24] It provided that "each republic . . . is a sovereign state" and that "the Union of Soviet Sovereign Republics is a sovereign, federative, democratic state." The treaty thus would have created layers of concurrent sovereignty. It provided that the Union and the republics would conjointly be full members of the international community. The sphere of joint authority of the Union and of the republics was to include the determination of the foreign policy of the USSR, control of the armed forces, and control of the Union state security system. The Union treaty would have been a treaty under the internal law of the USSR, and would probably have been a treaty also under international law. It contemplated that the center and the republics would share powers and that they would structure among themselves relations granting the republics more than autonomy/self-rule but less than full independence.

The center, under such an arrangement, would have become what is best described as a framework state for the quasi-independent or formally independent republics.[25] The Union treaty proposed a balance between power sharing, as practiced in the EC, and separatism, along the lines negotiated by Great Britain and the dominions when the British Commonwealth was created. It would have made it possible for all the republics

34   to seek admission to the UN and to become members alongside the Soviet Union, Ukraine, and Byelorussia. It is entirely possible that the treaty would have failed even if Gorbachev had prevailed. But with this caveat in mind, the treaty should be studied as an attempt to reconcile the claims of state unity with those of self-determination. The compromise operated on two levels: the domestic constitutional level and the international plane. The interest of the treaty is not that it attempted to salvage the communist empire, but that it addressed the problem of separatism in a fresh manner.

In an important respect, the proposed treaty failed to break new ground: it proceeded on the theory that the sovereignty of nations and the sovereignty of states must both have a *territorial* character.

★ ★ ★

Historically, the tie between sovereignty and territory is undeniable, except perhaps among nomadic peoples. Yet there was a time when sovereignty was divided, when secular sovereignty and religious sovereignty, for example, were in different hands.

The emergence of states with modified independence is not a novelty. The international order has exhibited great flexibility in granting state status to entities of all sorts. European statecraft has granted international standing to *sui generis* entities like the Holy See; to ministates like San Marino, Andorra, Liechtenstein, and Monaco; and to anomalous bodies like the Sovereign Order of the Knights of Malta. The Knights, for example, maintain diplomatic relations with a number of important Catholic countries in which they enjoy diplomatic privileges and immunities. These practices may have eased the proliferation of ministates and quasi-states in the years that followed the Second World War.

During the Cold War years, the UN dealt with the claims for self-determination of the peoples that were ruled by the European colonial powers but not by others. It did not address the claims of the nations ruled by the communist empire. It left unresolved the claims of the Quebecers, Corsicans, Basques, Sikhs, Kurds, and Palestinians. The existence of more than 6,000 linguistic groups points to the potential number of ethnic claims to come.

The coinage of independence has been devalued in the modern world. It is ironic that so many peoples clamor for it in an era in which the movement of capital, ideas, technologies, and persons has reduced the real significance of statehood, and when the sovereignty of states is steadily being eroded.

A NEW SPACE FOR NATIONS

The international system needs additional concepts and a richer vocabulary to accommodate the national claims that cannot be expressed within existing state structures. The international legal system lags behind the political and social realities in many countries. The contrast with the domestic legal order is striking. In the domestic order, new juridical concepts and instruments are commonplace. For instance, new forms of property and of credit have been given formal content and have transformed the character of the modern economy; credit cards and the trade in derivatives, in futures, in options, in repos, and in new securities have created new financial instruments, whose impact on society is

36   comparable only to that of the great technological innovations. They are in a real sense social inventions. They are, however, confined to the domestic arena. Yet this is a time when analogous "inventions" are needed in the international arena, as well.

It is possible to create a "new space" for nations that have not achieved independence without encouraging the forces of disintegration, of separatism and communal strife. A new space for nations would require a new status for such nations in international organizations and in international diplomacy. It would also require a willingness to move beyond—not to abandon, but to move beyond—the two methods traditionally used for meeting their concerns: the protection of minorities (with or without autonomy) and the protection of human rights.

What does a "new space for nations" mean? This term has both practical and theoretical connotations. Tinkering with the unity of states or modifying their sovereignty opens a Pandora's box of related issues. This involves not only the notions of sovereignty and of statehood, but also the concepts of self-determination, secession, nationhood, territory, and the exercise of individual rights and national rights. The relationships between these notions are both complex and variable. A new space for nations is an approach that tries to delink these issues, to deconstruct them into several components, and to reassemble them in a creative fashion. It involves an extension of the formal system of states to include alongside it a system of nations and peoples *that are not organized territorially into independent states*. This can take place in a manner that will not undermine the integrity of existing states.

The first requirement of this approach is to deconstruct the notion of sovereignty into two initial components: sovereignty as power over people and sovereignty as power over territory. A new space for nations would develop the concept of sovereignty over a people. Sovereignty over territory means final authority within a given territory (final in the sense that it precludes the right of any other power to exercise final authority).

The alternative to a territorially organized world is one in which there is no final authority of a territorial character or one in which there are no clear territorial boundaries. Interest in these alternatives is on the rise; they are by no means new. In conflicts over self-determination, territorial issues involve a choice between two approaches: one based on the creation of new boundaries, with the separation and, if need be, the transfer of populations (or the creation of minorities); and another based on functional boundaries and the disaggregation of sovereignty that allows populations to dwell where they are and to enjoy a full range of civil and political rights without territorial definition. The first approach is unitary, Jacobin,[26] and assimilationist; the other is decentralized and pluralist. Yet the connection between claims for self-determination and the control of territory is neither as clear-cut nor as uniform as some would argue.[27]

In the feudal state the attributes of sovereignty were not the monopoly of the king. Instead, an amalgam of authorities, towns, and monasteries exercised powers set by special customs and charters. In England the king's writ ran within defined limits; in medieval times the jurisdiction of the royal courts was strictly confined. A limited number of writs determined the remedies available from the Crown. Cities, manors, guilds, and monasteries enjoyed customs and privileges as a matter

38   of right; these were originally derived neither from the king nor from Parliament, although, as time went on, they were often confirmed by royal charters. In spiritual matters sovereignty was exercised by the Church, with its own system of ecclesiastical courts; in matters of craft it was exercised by the guilds. In France towns and provinces had the power to raise taxes and duties under long-established usage. The very phrase "custom duties" still points to an era in which duties were levied under such local customs. Allegiance was owed to regional lords, to royal overlords, and to the pope; it was owed to all concurrently. The boundaries that mattered changed for different purposes—for levying armies, collecting taxes, monopolizing commerce, and holding court.

During medieval times the affirmation of rights beyond territorial limits was not unusual. The Roman church, for example, continues to exercise its authority over believers without regard to frontiers. Medieval history provides a rich lore of concepts and practices in which authority was divided and sovereignty limited. Matters changed in 1789. The French Revolution introduced the concept of popular sovereignty that established the state as supreme over local laws and customs; it asserted the sovereignty of the state and affirmed its final authority over the national territory. No rights and privileges remained immune from the powers of the popular sovereign: all local rights and privileges could be rescinded and altered by it.

The process of the centralization of sovereignty in the state reached its climax earlier in this century. It is now being reversed. The deconstruction of sovereignty and the reallocation of its attributes is a key feature of the architecture of the new European Community. It reached new heights in the treaty of Maastricht.

Constructing a new space for ethnic groups and for nations claiming self-determination requires an integrated set of constitutional, regional, and international arrangements. These questions must be addressed on the international as well as on the domestic plane.

The international legal community can be broadened beyond states and international organizations to formally include peoples and nations.[28] Nations and peoples that have no state of their own can be recognized as such and endowed with an international legal status. Those that are politically organized could be given the right to be a party to different types of treaties and to take part in the work of international organizations. This status can be affirmed without calling into question the sovereignty of the states in which these nations and peoples dwell. What is required is for the international community to grant peoples organized on a nonterritorial basis a status similar to that of states, albeit limited to nonterritorial concerns. The extension of a legal personality to instrumentalities other than states is a recent phenomenon. Thus the International Court of Justice held that the United Nations Organization has the capacity to bring international claims. The Organization has, among states, a diplomatic standing similar to that of the states themselves. The EC is also recognized as having a legal standing separate from that of its members; it maintains active relations with many states. Only a few decades ago, the granting of legal status to organizations was regarded as a major innovation.

The further extension of legal personality to nonterritorially organized nations is still a utopian proposition. But it is a direction that states should consider as a technique for the management of ethnic conflicts and for the accommodation of ethnic diversity. In the United States several congressional committees have held hearings with the participation of Kurdish, Palestinian, Tibetan, and other representatives that did not prejudice the conduct of conventional foreign relations.

The United Nations could itself be used in some cases to moderate the intensity of ethnic conflicts by opening up new forms of participation for peoples and for nations. Under a somewhat futuristic scenario, the General Assembly could establish a new status of "Associated People of the United Nations" for nations that have no state of their own and that are politically organized in a democratic fashion. The members would negotiate the attributes of such status, which may include the right to address selected UN organs (without a vote) and to display flags and other symbols of nationality. Precedents exist for the creation of privileges without Charter amendment, such as those granted to observer missions. Nothing in the Charter is intrinsically incompatible with opening the Organization to the participation of national, ethnic, religious, and other groups. Many such groups have already had a hearing in different UN bodies. This can happen in a manner that, far from threatening the integrity of the states from which they hail, would reinforce their cohesion by providing a coveted outlet for the expression of *national* sentiments.

★ ★ ★

When a state is confronted with demands of a separatist character—for example, Canada in the case of Quebec—the territorial dimension of the dispute is of commanding importance: Will Quebec, its people and its territory, remain part of the Canadian state? In addressing a situation of this kind, the states-plus-nations approach involves a number of components.

First, an accord must outline terms for separation from an existing state and the new modalities of association (if any) with it. The accords setting up the CIS are a good illustration. These constitute the law of the new relationship between the parties. They outline how powers are divided or shared, and they define respective spheres of authority, competence, and jurisdiction. If the parties so desire, they can make provisions for a loose inclusive "framework" state or association in which they all join. Such a framework state can be made to retain some residual juridical sovereignty throughout the territory alongside the entities that constitute it.

Second, the terms of such an accord can be endorsed and guaranteed internationally by the Security Council or by other agencies, such as the EC. The accord may contemplate, for example, full diplomatic recognition of a framework state concurrently with that of its constituent members. It could also involve their participation in regional organizations. The acquiescence of powerful neighbors to changes in the status quo is evidently required if agreements are to prosper.

Third, it is possible to develop new forms of association between nations and states that need have no direct territorial implications. Political associations even of a federal or confederal character can be established between "peoples" and governmental agencies; they do not require the establishment of territorial entities. A great variety of forms of association is compatible with international practice. Associations can be functional (for example, the Bank of International Settlement), can be national (for example, the Palestine Liberation Orga-

42   nization), or can take any other shape that the parties desire. The Kurdish leader Jalal Talabani suggested, for instance, that the Kurds of northern Iraq establish special links with Turkey while remaining formally within the Iraqi state.

Separation through association can ease the friction of disunion. Association need not be invasive. It can be limited to mutually beneficial endeavors of an economic character, which is all that erstwhile hostile communities may agree to. Common regional instrumentalities, such as the CSCE, can confer status of symbolic significance. They open options for the participation of parties on the basis of equality. They make the indirect sharing of powers possible when a cutout between them is needed. For instance, some of the ethnic groups in Europe could be allowed to take part in the work of regional European organizations like the Council of Europe.

Juridical design is a variety of social architecture: it involves the conscious enlargement of the forms of legal order. It contrasts with the habitual juridical inquiry into what states have already consented to. Juridical design requires going beyond the bounds that international law traditionally recognizes.

NATIONAL HOME REGIMES

The notion of a special regime for a national home is new. Such a regime is meant as a comprehensive response to ethnic claims. It is designed primarily to reconcile the integrity and the sovereignty of states with the claims of national groups within them; to provide a context for common nationality links for nations that are divided by state boundaries; to address their yearning for national identity; and to do so without undermining the cohesion of multinational societies. Indeed, it is conceived to affirm the pluralistic nature of multinational societies. A "national home regime" also is concerned with national identity. Such a regime could provide the framework for defined individual rights for "nationals" within the limits of a home that would extend beyond national frontiers. Where two peoples contest the same territory, as in Bosnia, this concept could have made room—before the war broke out—for two national homes within a single territory. This is possible if a national home regime focuses on individual rights and on the disposition of land use questions at the local level.

The separation of the concepts of nationality and citizenship can be used creatively to remedy disputes about national identity, and to affirm the pluralistic character of a society. This separation goes against the practices of states that assimilate nationality and citizenship, as France does. A common nationality, distinct from state citizenship, can be used to express the common identity of the inhabitants of a national home, even one that stretches across state boundaries. A national home regime would permit the issuance of two sets of passports to the inhabitants of a country: a set of national passports to the inhabitants of the national-home areas, and set of citizenship passports to the citizens of the states. A common national passport could thus be issued to persons of diverse citizenships.

Some nations dwell among many states but retain a common identity. The Kurds are a prime example. Their aspiration to a national existence of their own was recognized in the Treaty of Sèvres which addressed the

44   disposition of Ottoman lands. The treaty was not ratified; it was superseded by the Treaty of Lausanne, which ignored the promises of the Sèvres blueprint. The Kurds are now dispersed in Iran, Turkey, Iraq, and Syria. This poses a challenge to the four states; it requires them to come to terms with Kurdish nationalism without undermining their own territorial integrity.

The distinct identity of a nation is often expressed in common cultural bonds and in an attachment to a common national home. The bond of nationality need not, and often does not, coincide with the bond of citizenship. Citizenship is a juridical concept derived from the state, whereas the bond of nationality is derived ethnically or culturally.[29] The common national home is a concept that has its roots in history, culture, and myth. The limits of a national home (*patrie* in French or *heimat* in German) are derived from ancient traditions rather than from juridical title.

FUNCTIONAL TERRITORIAL ARRANGEMENTS

With regard to territorial disputes, much new thinking is needed. The control of territory is broadly perceived as a zero-sum game. Hence, territorial disputes usually eschew creative solutions. More territory for one side normally means less for the other. It is believed that there is no way for territorial questions to be finessed and sidestepped. Frontiers must be established and property rights secured. Frontiers are designed to exclude and to set jurisdictional limits.

The concepts used in domestic territorial disputes and those invoked between states are strikingly different. The wealth and complexity of domestic practices is replaced internationally by simplistic and primitive notions of title and sovereignty. International practice conceives but of a limited set of limits to sovereignty. Its poverty is striking in contrast with the land law of England, for example, which, with its feudal background, allows a rich variety of solutions to the allocation of property rights. English land law is predicated on the notion that persons own not land, but a bundle of rights in the land. This bundle of rights can be disaggregated and divided both in time and in substance. Hence, estates can be crafted for different time periods and with different rights—life estates, estates in fee simple, and estates in fee tail, as well as leaseholds. The Roman law system is less flexible, but it does permit the carving of usufructuary rights and other servitudes.

The fundamental notion that title to territory involves a bundle of rights in the land rather than ownership of the land can be transplanted to the international arena. It lends itself to the design of territorial compromises of a functional nature. While the drawing of simple property limits is of great appeal and is most easily understood, it no longer corresponds to the realities of modern societies. In the life of modern cities, for example, ordinary property limits must be understood in the context of complex zoning regulations that govern the right to use and develop properties. Property limits are often less significant than the zoning restrictions that govern the property. Zoning regulations of all sorts are layered upon one another: for example, regulations on public use, density, residential and commercial use, street-level use, architectural features, and the height of buildings. Specialized agencies govern the restoration and maintenance of properties of historical interest; port authorities govern the development and management of

46   airports, ports, and bridges; park authorities govern the
development of public places; and public authorities can
invoke the right of eminent domain for public purposes.

In international relations, states can no longer use
their territory as they see fit in regard to environmental
matters, and a variety of special regimes have been
designed for specific territories. But the basic notions of
territorial sovereignty continue to invite the settlement
of territorial disputes in terms of simple boundary lines.

The notion of a national-home regime highlights
the complex nature of rights to territory in relations
between nations. This complexity is most evident in
diminutive territories where the land is claimed by two
or more nations. In such areas conventional territorial
compromises, in terms of a simple boundary line, present acute difficulties.

The idea that a single boundary line can be drawn
for all the purposes dictated by modern conditions continues to inform negotiations in the international arena.
This requires that a single line be drawn to meet the
vital security concerns of the parties and to set their
jurisdictional boundaries in all matters. It requires
that a single jurisdictional line be drawn for functions
as different as military defenses and access to water,
natural resources, fertile land, land for suburban development, holy sites, power stations, recreational space,
airspace, and the many other uses to which land is put in
modern times.

A functional approach to territorial disputes may
be particularly apt in situations in which different national communities are confined to small areas and in
which a single boundary line separating them would fail
to meet their fundamental requirements. A functional
approach involves the demarcation of different layers of

lines for different purposes. It gives a new meaning and practicality to the notion of territorial compromise. Thus, for example, the historic claims of a nation to a territory extending beyond its state limits could be expressed in terms that do not jeopardize the rights and the claims of its neighbors. Or, to take another example, lines drawn for security purposes need not coincide with other lines drawn for other purposes. The functional approach does not stand for any specific solution to territorial disputes; it is designed to make them more amenable to resolution. It also encourages the redistribution of competence in land use matters to the local level in order to reduce their contentiousness at the level at which national sensibilities are the most acute.

CHAPTER 3

From Ireland
to Yugoslavia

Nationalist movements that aim at independence
and aspire to remove other nations from lands
they claim have an edge over those that prefer a
pluralistic future. The resort to violence and terror is
within easy reach for the partisans of homogeneity. It is
a simple matter to provoke fear and hatred with crimes
that drive peoples and races apart. A demonstrated readiness to kill and the destruction of homes is a recipe for
ethnic separation. The persistence of violence against
civilians is an instrument for the establishment of
nonpluralistic entities. Territorially driven aspirations
to self-determination are prone to ugly excesses. The
crimes committed by the Serbian White Eagles in Bosnia since 1991 highlight the horrors of territorial
changes involving the forced transfer of populations.

The defense of pluralism is a much more delicate
affair. It requires first and foremost a conviction that
individual security and the security of the group are in
safe hands. Hence, in ethnic conflicts, the patterns in
which populations inhabit the land weigh heavily on the
range of their possible relationships. The conflicts
sparked by the dissolution of states where different nations and peoples dwell in ethnically homogeneous areas

can eventually be resolved by their separation on the ground. Whether they ultimately choose to associate and organize themselves in a common structure is another issue. In countries in which hostile ethnic groups live in distinct areas, partition and secession have a logic that is often compelling. This is not the case with territories in which nations are mingled with one another. In Bosnia, for example, Serbs, Muslims, and Croats lived in patterns of demographic promiscuity. This coexistence ended with the Serb onslaught and the flight of the Muslims. Conflicts in countries like Bosnia that involve an ethnic group whose demands are incompatible with any national or internal borders are the most difficult to manage.

To change the pattern in which populations mingle is to change the pattern of their future relationship. The separation of peoples can lead to partition, and once old fears abate, it can be patched up in a fragile federation. The preservation and the development of areas in which national groups mingle in safety with one another is a safeguard against the transfer of populations. This can lead to genuine association; but such areas remain hostage to the handlers of violence. What is at stake in the preservation of mixed territories is the establishment of patterns of coexistence that can be torn apart only at the greatest cost to all sides.

PEACEMAKING IN ETHNIC AND RELIGIOUS WARS

The relevance of a national home regime is most salient in three sets of situations: where ethnic separation has not taken place, where nations are divided by state boundaries, and where two peoples lay claim to the

50   same tract of land. But how "relevant" are mere ideas and concepts when much blood has been shed and where enemies are locked in mortal combat?

The role that "new ideas" and concepts can play in the settlement of long lasting wars must be viewed with realism and with a sense of proportion. The setting for peacemaking in ethnic wars is both grim and discouraging. Political efforts are invariably situated in the context of long and complex local histories of strife, of grievances, and of crimes well remembered. Layers upon layers of promises ignored, broken pledges, and treaties violated form the usual background to new promises, new pledges, and new treaties offered. Outside powers and third parties are, more often than not, believed to manipulate local politics for their own ends. Wariness, extremism, and stridency nourish the fears that cruel tragedies sustain. The fragility of a status quo is often preferable to the anxieties of untried relationships with a hated adversary. The temptation to commit violence—as well as to reduce the other side to subservience once and for all—is tempered by the experience of past failures. The power of terror and of gruesome acts to cut the road to compromise is well tested. Intransigence and extremism reinforce arguments to postpone a settlement until a better correlation of forces prevails so that it is possible to negotiate from strength. On the other hand, when confidence is high, the need for compromise is not apparent. The problems of peacemaking are compounded where the claims of justice are taken to weigh more heavily in favor of one side than of the other; feelings of justice aggrieved prey on the minds of victims and of neutrals alike. Moralistic arguments feed partisan advocacy and sustain bias in the outside world, as well as intransigence among enemies. It is even worse when the clash is between two sets of just causes. Condemned communities bask in feelings of isolation and in the determination to hold out. Media wars waged with the lure of money and of profitable connections feed biased reporting shrouded in principle and moralism. Thus, the media unwittingly fortify cynicism and encourage posturing. The media themselves become an arena of strife.

Weary diplomats are familiar with complicated and sometimes clever schemes for future arrangements. The problem, in their view, is not the lack of blueprints, but the absence of political will. Once the will is there, a way can be found, they believe, to hammer out a compromise.

When conflicts become chronic and nasty, the temptation is to sit back and await the arrival of this political will, for statesmen who engage in negotiations with a slender chance of success have little to gain and risk a great deal. What brings this will about varies with the circumstances: the rise of a new generation, shifts in political alignments, and other unpredictable events.

The task of statesmanship is to nurture the emergence of that will. This requires consummate skill in structuring choices for all sides that will induce them to enter the labyrinth of give-and-take. It also requires the design of a vision of something at the end of the labyrinth that all sides can live with. This vision must not require contending sides to disown the cause for which they made painful sacrifices or to renege on cherished goals. But this vision must not be so specific as to spell out what the parties alone should be expected to craft in tedious negotiations among themselves.

The role of new ideas and concepts is thus most evident at two levels: they should provide an encourage-

52   ment for negotiations to begin, and they should set the tone and context for them to continue once they are under way. They can be useful in the prenegotiation phase, and they can be fruitful when talks begin. But they should at no point be allowed to complicate negotiations that have already begun.

The ethnic conflicts in Ireland, Iraq, the Caucasus, and elsewhere have one thing in common: an obsessive preoccupation with issues of sovereignty, of statehood, and of national identity. They touch on concepts that were forged in the political culture of the Western world. The brief survey that follows is not meant to cover the entire world, but concentrates on a few conflicts in Europe and the Near East. It is meant to highlight the recurrence of a narrow roster of issues in conflicts that undermine the stability of the international order.

NORTHERN IRELAND

For the first time since Ireland became independent in 1922, representatives of the Irish government met in June 1992 with officials of Protestant and of Catholic political parties in the North and with representatives of the British government. Participants included the hardline Protestant leader Ian Paisley, but excluded representatives of the Sinn Fein, the political wing of the Irish Republican Army, because it refuses to forswear violence in its struggle to unify the island. The talks are part of a phased process to address the structure of a new government for Northern Ireland. They recessed in November 1992 for elections in the Republic and in Ulster. Since 1970, more than 3,000 persons have been killed in the conflict over this territory.

An estimated 950,000 Protestants and 650,000 Catholics reside in the province. The Catholic share of the population is rising fast; Catholics now form 43 percent of the population in the North. This demographic surge is putting pressure on the Protestant majority. The Protestant side insists on continued union with Britain. Most Catholics, but not all, demand closer links with Ireland. In 1974 the government in Westminster took over direct rule in the province to control the communal violence.

In their June 1992 meeting, the leaders of Northern Ireland's principal Protestant and Catholic political parties agreed to form a committee to consider how to establish a new local government in the North. The Catholic nationalists of the Social Democratic and Labor party proposed a local government arrangement with formal roles for both Ireland and the EC. The Protestant Unionists wanted to break the 1985 Anglo-Irish Agreement, which they maintain gives Ireland the right to interfere in the internal affairs of the North. They proposed power sharing between local Protestants and Catholics, but without any role for the Dublin government. They insisted that the agenda for the talks include possible changes in article 2 of the 1937 Irish Constitution, which says, "The national territory consists of the whole island of Ireland, its islands and the territorial seas." In 1985 the Irish government conceded that "any change in the status of Northern Ireland would only come about with the consent of a majority of the people of Northern Ireland." The claim to sovereignty of the United Kingdom is formulated in the Government of Ireland Act of 1920, the Ireland Act of 1949, and a set of Northern Ireland Constitution acts. The United Kingdom's position is that the 1985 Anglo-Irish Agreement

54   does not qualify its sovereignty; the position of the Irish courts is that the agreement does not qualify the claim of the Republic. The short-lived 1992 talks were a breakthrough of sorts; they were perhaps the biggest political step since Northern Ireland was established. In early 1993 the new Irish foreign minister signaled that Ireland might be willing to consider changes in the Constitution.

The time may be at hand, seventy years after the independence of Ireland, to move toward a resolution of this appalling conflict. This will be another long, drawn-out effort. The routine of hatred and violence is well entrenched, and there are vested interests for its continuation. Psychological habits are hard to break, and confrontational language difficult to change. The struggle is neither purely religious, though echoes of religious coercion linger, nor purely nationalistic, though British forces appear to some as an army of occupation. The virulence of the conflict and the depth of hatreds are hard for outsiders to fathom.

The right political and economic leverage can perhaps now be brought to bear on all sides.[1] Yet more is needed. There must be a vision of how to reconcile the irreconcilable: the claims of union and of partition, the claims for the unity of Ireland and the choice of the majority of Ulster's inhabitants to remain in the United Kingdom. Without such a vision, every step toward a compromise can be attacked as the betrayal of martyrs and of ideals that the generation of the fathers was willing to die for.

During his election campaign, President Clinton proposed to send a peace envoy to Northern Ireland. In early 1993 the British government indicated that it would accept an official U.S. fact-finding mission to

Northern Ireland, but insisted—for good reason—that progress would come only when the multiparty peace talks resumed.

The concept of a national home regime can be relevant here. A superficial and crude sketch of this notion could sustain and nourish the political will of the parties to move to serious negotiations. This notion is not a specific blueprint for a settlement, but rather a vision for what such a blueprint may aim at. No ideas or set of ideas are going to resolve a conflict that has endured for centuries, but they can help restore flexibility to long hardened positions. In simple terms, a national home regime would introduce a third component—so as to transform the either/or nature of the union-partition contest. This could open up a fresh menu of bridging ideas from which all might draw some comfort.

A rough sketch suffices here: an Irish national home to be established for the whole of the Irish isles; to be established not in lieu of, but in addition to, the existing Irish Republic and the province of Northern Ireland. This would leave the links between Great Britain and Northern Ireland unimpaired. This formula is consistent with the provisions of the Irish Constitution, with the positions of the Ulster Protestants, and with Ireland's 1985 commitment to the view that the status of the North can be changed only with the agreement of its inhabitants.

An Irish national home could provide a framework for a new all-Irish national authority, with authority over matters of common concern to the Republic and to the *Catholic* inhabitants in the North who wish to be included. It could, moreover, provide the framework for other agreed links between municipal government

56   authorities that so choose and other authorities south of
the border.

An Irish national home would not affect the Protestant majority in Northern Ireland; neither Protestants'
rights nor their citizenship nor their participation in the
Parliament in London would be modified. The powers
of the new local government in Belfast would not be
abridged. The Dublin authorities would have no powers
over Ulster as a whole. In contrast to the provisions of
the Anglo-Irish Agreement of 1985, the links between
the Republic and the North would affect the latter's
Catholic inhabitants only, rather than concern the province as a whole. The jurisdiction of the London government in Ulster would be defined functionally to govern
such matters as security and other powers that would
not be exercised by the local government in Belfast.
Internationally, the government in London would continue to speak for Ulster and for the citizens of the
United Kingdom and Northern Ireland. Moreover, the
membership of the United Kingdom and of Eire in the
EC can facilitate arrangements linking the sides in some
common instrumentalities in which the Community
can be invited to play a role.

The conflict and the tensions between the two sides
is felt most acutely at the local level, and it is at this level
that practical and symbolic solutions might help. The
Catholic and the Protestant neighborhoods of the larger
cities might be given a degree of submunicipal autonomy analogous to that enjoyed by the *contradas* in the
medieval city of Siena. It will be recalled that Constant-
inople, in Byzantine times, was a metropolis with separate districts and virtual cities for the different nations
that lived and traded there: the Genoese, the Venetians,
and others were granted a wide measure of religious and

judicial autonomy. With these images in mind, it should be possible to construct arrangements to devolve jurisdiction over real estate and police matters, for example, to the local and submunicipal levels. The devolution of powers to grass-roots authorities might reduce the salience of power sharing between Protestants and Catholics in the provincial government that is so redolent with constitutional issues.

Furthermore, an Irish national home would help develop any needed concepts of national identity with a better fit for the existing territorial arrangements. Such identity concepts could be introduced to the advantage of all sides. The negotiators alone are in a position to decide whether to add issues to a crammed and difficult agenda in order to enhance the fluidity of negotiations that can stall on matters on which the parties' positions are too well entrenched. The virtue of adding new issues is to bring up subjects on which the sides had no opportunity to take hard positions. Fresh issues can create grounds for agreement where none existed before.

National identity with a better fit for the territorial realities on the island would flow from two sources: the identity that flows from state citizenship and the identity that flows from the common bond of nationality. The two kinds of identity are separate from one another. Each would be expressed in differentiated forms of political participation in the life of the Irish national home and in British political life. Each would be evidenced in passports and in other identity papers confirming status rights. The Catholics in the North could be granted, as Irish nationals (not to be confused with Irish citizens), specific rights pertaining to the national home in the Republic. An Irish national passport (distinct from a citizenship passport) could be made available on request

58 to the inhabitants of Eire and to the Catholics in the North. As Irish nationals, they could be given the right to participate in the political life of the Republic on an equal footing with its citizens.

There is no theoretical obstacle to giving all Irish nationals in the province a choice between citizenship in the United Kingdom and in Eire. This could be done without requiring them to forfeit rights acquired as citizens of the United Kingdom. The Dublin government can be given the authority to speak both domestically and internationally for all Irish nationals who inhabit any part of Ireland, or any other country, for that matter.

An approach of this nature would restore the symbolic unity of Ireland, as an internationally recognized "National Home of the Irish Nation," without prejudice to the existing status of Eire and of Northern Ireland. The EC could be invited to contribute to such an arrangement by making room in some European institutions for representatives of the Irish national home to be seated alongside those of Ireland and the United Kingdom. The cumulation of arrangements of this nature should erode the hard-and-fast line that separates partition from union.

These notions cannot by themselves unlock the gate to agreement between the communities. Used wisely, however, they might help set the tone for negotiations that will neither be brief nor easily shatter the ideological barrier of indivisible sovereignty.

CYPRUS

It will surprise no one that the problem on the island of Cyprus differs fundamentally from the Irish question.

The peoples, cultures, religions, history, and expectations are different. Nevertheless, there is a unifying thread: the preoccupation with a similar roster of issues—sovereignty, statehood, partition, union, and national identity.

In contrast to most peoples, the majority of Cypriots considered independence to be the second-best solution rather than their first choice. The call for *enosis*, or union with Greece, continues to echo in the politics of the 550,000 Greek Cypriots, even though in a much muted form. In 1963 the attempt of President Makarios to "amend" the constitution signified the virtual abandonment of the carefully crafted compromise of the 1960 Zurich agreements and the collapse of the constitutional order of the island. It ushered in a period of violence between the two communities and a growing intervention by the regime of the colonels in Athens. On July 15, 1974, the Athens junta fomented a coup against Makarios, who escaped to New York to plead with the Security Council for an end to Greek intervention. These events precipitated the intervention of the Turkish army five days later.

Before the Turkish intervention, the 120,000 Turkish Cypriots constituted less than 20 percent of the total island population. The present size of the Turkish-speaking population is not known; many Turkish Cypriots have emigrated, but a significant number of Turkish settlers from the mainland have arrived since the Turkish intervention in 1974. That intervention led to the displacement of some 150,000 Greek Cypriot and 45,000 Turkish Cypriot inhabitants. The separation of Greek and Turkish inhabitants is now all but complete. The establishment of the Turkish Republic of Northern Cyprus (internationally largely unrecognized) in the

60   years that followed the Turkish landing did not close the
door to the possible reunification of the island. On both
sides, the contest between the forces of union and of
separation continues.

Ultimately, the relations between the governments
in Athens and Ankara are likely to determine what
progress can be made in the drawn-out talks with the
Greek and Turkish Cypriot leaders that have taken place
under the aegis of the UN. The two metropolitan governments ought to have an interest in resolving the
Cyprus dispute, since each faces other problems of
greater magnitude. From a Turkish perspective, Cyprus
is not a priority issue; but it is not one that Turkey can
neglect. The personal influence of Raouf Denktash, the
Turkish Cypriot leader, and the resonance of Turkish
resistance to Greek domination are factors in Turkish
domestic politics. Turkey is at the junction of some of
the world's most ominous problems.[2] It is preoccupied
with the campaign against the Kurdish Workers' Party
(PKK) rebels and with the war in the former Yugoslavia. Iranian and Arab volunteers are involved there.
The war has deepened the chasm between the Christian
world and the world of Islam at a time when Ankara is
kept waiting at the door of the EC. Religious passions
are rising throughout the Muslim world and beyond.
The conflicts in the Balkans and in the Caucasus, which
pit Christian and Muslim populations against one another, can only strengthen religious sentiment in Turkey
and worry an elite committed to the secular legacy of the
Ataturk Revolution. The clash between Armenia and
the Turkic peoples of Azerbaijan threatens to align Turkey and Russia on opposite sides. The Kurdish problem,
the grave situation in Iraq, the murky ambitions of the
Damascus regime, and the growing might of Iran are

added major concerns, even though relations with the Teheran regime remain fairly cordial.[3] In this difficult environment, the military in Ankara are not likely to accept a situation in which hostile Greek forces on Cyprus can be allowed to have most of mainland Turkey within easy missile range. Turkish officials have nevertheless expressed a readiness to withdraw Turkish troops from Cyprus as part of an overall settlement on the island.

From a Greek perspective, Turkey and its perceived territorial ambitions loom large. Athens still takes the Turkish landing on Cyprus in 1974 as proof of Turkish expansionist designs. Greece, however has more reason to worry about the turn of events in the Balkans. Athens must fear that the war between Serbia and its neighbors may spread to the province of Kosovo and embroil the Muslims of Albania, triggering an uncontrollable flow of refugees. The Greek government is intensely concerned with the events in Macedonia and with that former Yugoslav republic's efforts to obtain international recognition. The Macedonian question continues to arouse much popular emotion in Greece. Athens is also concerned about Thrace and about its Muslim citizens there.

The deteriorating situation in the Balkans should be a strong incentive in Athens to improve relations with Ankara. The rare coincidence of Turkish and Greek worries about the Balkans, about the Caucasus, and about the Middle East is a favorable setting for a resolution of the dispute on Cyprus. Ankara and Athens can be expected to urge the island leaders to reach an accord. Current efforts to settle the Cyprus dispute build on the painstaking efforts of the new UN secretary-general, Boutros Boutros-Ghali. In a book

62   written before the 1992 round of negotiations, former
U.S. Ambassador to Greece Monteagle Stearns wrote:

> In fact the broad outlines of what a final settlement of the Cypriot
> inter-communal problems would look like have been clear for a long
> time. Pérez de Cuéllar seems to have annoyed both sides by spelling
> them out. . . . Cyprus is the common home of the Greek Cypriot
> community and of the Turkish Cypriot community. Their relation-
> ship is not one of majority and of minority, but one of two commu-
> nities in the State of Cyprus. . . . The two communities
> have . . . specifically rejected as options union in whole or in part
> with any other country and any form of partition or secession. The
> two communities have stated that they wish to establish a federation
> that is bicommunal as regards the constitutional aspects and bi-zonal
> as regards the territorial aspects.[4]

A "set of ideas" negotiated under the auspices of
the secretary-general of the UN is the basis for the
current negotiations between the two sides.[5] It envisions
a Cypriot Federal Republic would be established with
two states, one Greek and the other Turkish. The text
contemplates the unity of Cyprus as one state; this state
would be given substance in the international arena
rather than in the domestic arrangement, which would
have a bizonal character. The new accord would ban the
division of the island, as well as any future unification
with either Greece or Turkey.

The "set of ideas" also stipulates that Cyprus is
"the Homeland" of the Greek Cypriot and of the Turkish Cypriot communities. Under the terms of a new
constitution that the two sides are expected to negotiate,
the powers to be vested in the federal government will
be limited to foreign affairs, central bank functions,
international trade, defense within the context of alli-
ances and guarantee agreements, federal budget, justice,
police, health, and other essential tasks of a functional
character. The suggested federal powers are molded on
the Swiss rather than on the American model; they are

of a *confederal* character, even though the language of the text is federal in nature. The draft is consistent with the desire of the two communities to live separate lives. The political equality of the two sides would not mean equal participation in all the bodies of the federal government.

Difficult problems abound: the return of displaced persons; the boundaries between the two zones; the percentage, and quality, of the island's land to be retained by the Turkish side; the status of special areas, such as Morphou; and the continued presence of foreign troops. The Turkish Cypriot side still questions the readiness of the Greek community to accept the full implications of a bicommunal and bizonal constitution. It insists that the bicommunal character of the island be given expression in the arena of foreign relations. It also demands an electoral system that does not formally preclude the election of a Turkish Cypriot as federal president. The issue of the boundaries of the Turkish zone remains in dispute.

President George Vassiliou gave his support to the "set of ideas" and campaigned for reelection on that basis. His narrow defeat by the veteran Cypriot statesman Glafcos Clerides in the March 1993 polls was widely interpreted as a repudiation of these ideas. Clerides wants to see them modified. The Turkish Cypriot leadership continues to express grave reservations about them as well. Denktash contests the priority assigned to territorial matters by Boutros-Ghali while major constitutional issues remain pending. The problem of the rotation of powers between the Greek Cypriot president and the Turkish Cypriot vice president has not been resolved. Each side is eager to have the other concede the legitimacy of what it has done after the failure of the previous constitutional arrangements. After his elec-

64   tion, Clerides indicates he would ask for a postponement of the talks that had been scheduled for the spring of 1993 at the UN.

The Greek Cypriots continue to regard the Turkish occupation as the paramount issue, together with the return of territories and of displaced persons. While most political forces appear disposed to live with bicommunal and bizonal arrangements, ecclesiastical and right-wing circles remain committed to restore the Hellenic character of the island as a whole; but their influence is waning, and their candidate did not muster more than 18 percent of the popular vote in the first round of the February 1993 presidential elections. The astonishing prosperity of the Greek side, which has grown at an annual rate of 7 percent of GNP since 1988, stands in contrast to the stagnating economy of the Turkish Republic of Northern Cyprus (TRNC). Both communities have adjusted to the division of the island, and many have benefited from it; the status quo is decried everywhere, but its comforts are evident on both sides of the green line.

Nevertheless, both Clerides and Denktash affirm an underlying commitment to find a settlement. That commitment is sustained on the Greek side by hopes to join the EC and by the aspiration to regain lost lands and properties. The Turkish side is moved by a desire to end its isolation and to infuse a new life in the local economy, which has been hurt by the boycott on trade and tourism. On the Turkish side, however, influential politicians have staked their future and their plans for economic growth on the permanent division of the island and on the separate development of their unrecognized republic, which in the meantime is increasingly integrated with mainland Turkey.

If the political will to find a settlement persists, it
should remain possible to overcome disagreements on
constitutional issues and on issues of governance as part
of a package that would include the concrete questions
of territorial limits and of the rights of displaced persons.[6] With regard to constitutional aspects, a wide
menu of solutions remains plausible: the rotation of
some of the powers of the presidency, rather than the
rotation of the office itself; the establishment of an additional office for the vice president, to enhance his international standing and to entrench his participation in the
international relations of Cyprus; and new systems of
weighted direct voting, to meet the demands of the
Turkish side that members of their community not be
formally barred from the highest office in the land.
Moreover, the staged application of a revised "set of
ideas" according to a staggered timetable could open
additional vistas for compromise: an early application
for international purposes only, and a later one for domestic matters. It could be coupled with provisions for a
return to the status quo ante in the event of a failure in
the negotiations.

The protection of the Turkish and of the Greek
areas of the island is a real issue; the intercommunal
conflict has traumatized both sides. The 1960 Treaties of
Guarantee and of Alliance contemplated the continued
presence in Cyprus of small metropolitan Greek and
Turkish contingents. The 1960 Treaty of Guarantee
provided that each of the guarantor powers—Greece,
Turkey, and the United Kingdom—could take unilateral action to carry out its commitments if concerted
action between them and the Republic of Cyprus proved
impossible. The Greek Cypriot side maintains that its
interpretation of the Treaty of Guarantee is different,

66 and that guarantor powers do not and cannot have a unilateral right of military intervention, since such unilateral intervention would conflict with their UN Charter obligations. The guarantor powers will presumably be called upon again to be the guarantors of last resort, as they were under the 1960 treaty. Under the "set of ideas," metropolitan military contingents on the island would be reduced. Arrangements could conceivably be made to incorporate the remaining forces in a regional structure under the auspices of the CSCE or, conceivably, even of NATO. They would be expected to retain the capacity to interpose their units in the event the physical security of either community is threatened and in the event local forces cannot assure their safety.

Prospects for a settlement remain contingent upon a heightened feeling of security among the inhabitants on both sides of the green line who were victims of the violent events of the past and who watch with foreboding the savagery of the Yugoslavian wars, as well as on a shared vision of the future that is more appealing to them than the present division. In November 1992 Secretary-General Boutros-Ghali decided to rebuke the Turkish Cypriot negotiators: "I have found that the positions of the Turkish Cypriot side are fundamentally at variance with the set of ideas under three broad headings: (a) the concept of the federation; (b) displaced persons; and (c) territorial adjustments."[7] He noted pointedly that Security Council resolution 774 indicated that the current negotiating effort cannot continue indefinitely, and that it requested that he recommend alternative courses of action should the sides fail to reach an agreement. It is difficult to assess the impact that Boutros-Ghali's stark disagreement with Denktash—

on the very concept of the federation—will have on the course of negotiations.

A disavowal of the painfully crafted "set of ideas" could well lead the international community—which is beset by far more urgent problems—to a policy of benign neglect of the Cyprus dispute; to acquiescence in the division of the island; and to a gradual acceptance of a separate sovereign entity in the present Turkish Cypriot enclave closely integrated with the mainland. There are reasons to hope that President Clerides will seek a direct understanding with his opposite number, President Denktash, with whom he has had a long relationship. Both accept the principles underlying the set of ideas. They share a resistance to the imperious intrusiveness of the secretary-general in their island's affairs. They may attempt to work things out with a less-salient UN role.

THE FORMER YUGOSLAVIA

The deficiencies of a territorial approach to ethnic disputes, involving the separation of populations, are painfully evident in the former Yugoslavia. The rapid tide of events, the carnage, and the massive flight of populations expelled from their towns and villages continue unabated. The tectonic plates of different civilizations collide in the Balkans. Few areas of the world are more deeply scarred by a coincidence of ethnic, religious, historical, cultural, and political fault lines.

The Yugoslav conflict exemplifies the tension between several principles: the principles of self-determination, nonintervention in domestic strife, the inviolability of territorial frontiers, and respect for hu-

68   man rights and the rights of minorities. Here, as in Ireland and in Cyprus, political discourse is redolent with references to unity and partition, to sovereignty, and to independence.

In 1991 the armed resistance of the Serbian-dominated Yugoslav National Army (JNA) to the secession of Slovenia and of Croatia presented the European states with a hard choice between support for self-determination and for the territorial integrity of states. The commitment of the European nations to the preservation of the territorial status quo in Europe was the foundation of the Helsinki Final Act of 1975 and of the CSCE process that followed. In imposing sanctions on Serbia, the Security Council reaffirmed the principle that borders must be altered not by force but by agreement only.

Germany leaned strongly in favor of the right to self-determination in Croatia and in Slovenia, true to its strong historical ties with these nations, last manifested in the Nazi era. France, together with the United Kingdom, Spain, and Greece, labored to hold Yugoslavia together as one state, albeit in a looser confederation. Initially France was true to its own historical ties with Serbia even in little things. For instance, its representative in the Security Council wanted to exempt Serbian sporting activities from the sanctions the Council voted. France, Spain, and the United Kingdom are concerned not to set precedents that could prove troublesome in the handling of their own separatist movements—in Corsica, in the Basque region, in Scotland, and in Northern Ireland. German Chancellor Helmut Kohl observed that some EC countries had considerable problems with separatist ideas in their own countries and were more interested in projecting any decisions over Yugoslavia to their situations back at home. As the conflict in Yugoslavia intensified, it became clear that while the Serbian-dominated JNA was initially used to defend the Federal Union, it rapidly became an instrument, together with local militias, for carving out territorial enclaves for the Serbs in Slovenia and in Croatia. This was before the war spread to Bosnia in 1992, when the heinous features of Serbian aggression became apparent to the whole world.

At one time, it seemed that the Serb leadership in Belgrade was prepared to consider nonterritorial solutions for the Serbs in Croatia. Serbia had agreed to respect Croatia's right to independence within existing borders in return for giving the Serbs in Croatia a special protected status. This was a legitimate issue. In a country in which the ethnic hatreds and division fed by memories of the Second World War and by religious antagonisms easily lead to unspeakable atrocities—from which none of the sides can be absolved—the protection and security of minorities is a matter of life and death.

The ethnic-religious-civil-international conflict taking place in the former Yugoslav Federal Republic is being waged in large part for territorial stakes. With the support of the Belgrade government, the Bosnian Serbs are carving out areas of Bosnia in the crudest way—by murdering and expelling Muslim inhabitants. The pursuit of self-determination for Serbs and for Croats is conceived in territorial terms. The atrocities inherent in efforts to "cleanse" areas of other ethnic groups are predictable where self-determination is meant to exclude minorities. The widespread killings in Bosnia were perpetrated when Muslim populations were forced out of their towns and villages, and not only during the shelling of Sarajevo. A policy of ethnic homogeneity in a country in which peoples and commu-

70   nities have long lived side by side must bring horror on a large scale, on the model of what happened in Lebanon.

In Bosnia elements of the JNA lent support to local Serbian militias, perhaps in the hope of uniting areas under their control with Serbia. The territorial design behind Serbian moves was evident in the carving of a land corridor in northern Bosnia to link Belgrade with the so-called Serbian Republic in the Croatian area of Krajina. In Belgrade political support for a Greater Serbia remained strong as the UN sanctions took hold. Furthermore, Serbian popular hostility to minorities remained so entrenched that support for minority rights meant a certain electoral death.[8]

Serb aspirations take many forms, some benign and others less so. They include all but faded hopes for a restructuring of the former Yugoslav federal state as a looser confederation; the union of Serbia with other Serb lands in neighboring states into a Greater Serbia; the partition of these states; territorial autonomy for Serbs living outside Serbia; the expulsion of other ethnic groups from Serb areas in Bosnia; and the formation of homogeneous ethnic enclaves.

The restoration of peace in Bosnia will require a new system of relations among Serbs, Muslims, and Croats, based on an end to the massive forcible transfer of populations. These transfers have exposed multitudes to death and to starvation during the bitter winter months.

Any arrangement will have to come to terms with the patterns of ethnic settlement, with the fact that in Bosnia, Muslims, Croats, and Serbs used to live in mixed communities. For all practical purposes the Serbs have achieved their war aims in Bosnia; they have separated the communities with a brutality that makes a return to earlier forms of coexistence difficult in the extreme. Despite recognition by the EC and by the United States, the republic of Bosnia-Herzegovina had, by the end of 1992, almost ceased to exist. President Radovan Karadzic, of the self-proclaimed Serbian Republic of Bosnia, declared that while he controls 70 percent of the country's territory, he claims "only" 64 percent for the Serbs, who make up less than one-third of the original population of 4.35 million inhabitants. The success of the Serbs is manifest (even if it is true, as the Bosnian leader maintains, that the Serbs control "only" 55 percent of his country's territory). The land grab by the Croats must be added to that of the Serbs to appreciate the problems facing the government in Sarajevo. It retains control of a small sliver of territory in and near Sarajevo and of a few isolated patches. More than a quarter of the population have been driven away from their homes. The rout was so complete that President Alija Izetbegovic had backed the idea of placing Bosnia-Herzegovina under some form of UN protectorate to help reconstitute the Bosnian government and to restore its authority over the whole country.

The demographic pattern that existed before the war began cannot be restored. The atrocities committed during that conflict preclude the large scale return of victims to live alongside the perpetrators. The desire of the inhabitants to return to their homes will for a long time be checked by their fears of life among enemies. The idea that Bosnia can endure as a unitary state has been crushed. The international identity of Bosnia is a matter of secondary concern to its inhabitants when so much of its population remains at risk.

George Shultz has eloquently defined the issue in Bosnia.[9] It is, he has said, first and foremost a human-

72   itarian one. The horrors have to stop, and the population has to be helped. More fundamentally, however,
the problem is how to govern diversity. The warring
nations perceive it a little differently: how to survive on
one's land without being ruled or dominated by hated
neighbors. In the past, the answers given to this problem were often simple and terrible. Ethnic cleansing and
the exchange or transfer of populations are no novelty.
A similar process took place between Greece and Turkey
in the 1920s, major episodes occurred in India and in
Pakistan in 1947, and the expulsion of the Jews was an
often repeated policy of the Christian kings of Europe.

The London Conference on Yugoslavia convened
in the fall of 1992, under the leadership of Cyrus Vance,
the former U.S. secretary of state, and Lord Owen, the
former British foreign secretary. It combined the peacekeeping diplomacy of the UN and the peacemaking
efforts of the EC that Lord Carrington had conducted.
Six special steering committees were set up, including
the Minority Task Force, to establish a consistent approach to minorities throughout the former Yugoslavia.[10] That committee decided to address the status of
ethnic Albanian majorities in the Serb-controlled province of Kosovo and in the province of Macedonia, and
the status of ethnic Hungarians in Voyvodina and of
Muslims in the Sandjak.

The problem confronting Vance and Owen was a
harsh one: What could be done in a situation in which
neither the European states nor the newly elected Clinton administration contemplated rolling back the Serbs
and forcing them to disgorge their territorial gains?
What could be done about Serbian conquests and the
acquisition of territories by the heinous policy of ethnic
cleansing? What could be done in a situation in which

lifting the arms embargo to supply the Muslims would probably widen the war and jeopardize the security of the peacekeeping forces? What could be done in a situation in which the Serbs are left with an overwhelming advantage in heavy weapons? What could be done about Serb leaders who have been characterized as "war criminals" even by the previous American secretary of state? The answer of Vance and Owen was a plan that calls for the Serbs to withdraw from some, but not all, of the lands they conquered, and to trust that a credible UN or NATO peacekeeping force, with U.S. ground forces—and perhaps also with Russian troops—will be able to prevent Serb violations of a territorial agreement that has yet to be finalized. Vance and Owen developed a constitutional framework to divide Bosnia into ten autonomous provinces and to recast it as a decentralized state with most governmental functions carried out by its provinces.[11] Three of these provinces would have an ethnic Muslim majority, three would have an ethnic Croat majority, and three would have an ethnic Serb majority; Sarajevo and its region would have a special status. Neither the Bosnian Serbs nor the Bosnia government in Sarajevo has accepted the plan. Only the Croats have been willing to sign on. The Bosnian Serbs object to the plan because it requires them to surrender hard-fought territorial gains beyond the 64 percent of Bosnian lands in private Serb ownership, the Bosnian leader Izetbegovic objects to a map that would legitimize Serb conquests.

The Vance-Owen formulas for a decentralized Bosnian state seek to reconcile the principle that aggression and ethnic cleansing cannot prevail with the fact that there is no way to restore Bosnia to its condition before the onslaught of the Serbs. The international life

74 of the state of Bosnia has been brief—it began in the spring of 1992 with recognition by the EC and the United States. Marshal Tito had originally set the borders of Bosnia so as to include a sizable Serb population to balance the Muslims. In the winter of 1993, the Vance-Owen plan proposed that a three-party administration, rather than the present government, assure the transition under the plan. The plan succeeded in having the Serbs give up their aspiration to establish a separate Bosnian Serb state, but there is considerable unease about the ultimate ambitions of the Serbs. The constitutional framework that all three sides have accepted provides that "the provinces shall not have any international legal personality and may not enter into agreements with foreign States or with international organizations."

Nothing in the Vance-Owen plan can alter the fact that ethnic links will persist across the provincial borders into Serbia and Croatia. But the plan takes no formal account of this fact. The recognition of such ties, without prejudice to the integrity of the states in Yugoslavia, should be an ingredient of a permanent solution. The creation of new kinds of links and of union among nations and peoples on the one hand, and between nations and states on the other, could hold one of the keys to a reordering of the former Yugoslavia. This could be achieved through the establishment of functional associations of peoples alongside associations of states as suggested by the states-plus-nations approach.

The elaborate jigsaw map devised by Vance and Owen offers local ethnic majorities a wide measure of self-rule. Constitutional provisions and international monitoring and control devices would assure the protection of the ethnic minorities in these provinces, but these minority groups would remain subject to provincial police forces answerable to the provincial governments dominated by one of the other groups.

Underlying the Vance-Owen proposals is a classic single-line territorial approach. A single-line approach involves the demarcation of one line—in this case, the provincial border—for virtually all functional purposes (security, jurisdictional, legislative, cultural, and economic). The exception is the limited governmental functions to be carried out by the central government in the decentralized state. These proposals, which eschew the division of Bosnia into ethnic cantons, and which repudiate the policies of ethnic cleansing, nevertheless have a strong partitionist flavor. But like all single-line proposals, they might exacerbate, rather than calm, local strife. Local criminal acts against minorities—cold-blooded stabbings, ax murders, and the like—might escape the net of constitutional safeguards and "control devices" contemplated in the plan.

A states-plus-nations approach, on the other hand, would have given preference to the delimitation of a variety of boundary lines and functional borders for different purposes. It would have provided for local security arrangements and for a variety of jurisdictional limits, to give the minorities tangible protection with local militias of their own. This is not to say—without further investigation—that a settlement with tiered functional lines would in fact be possible in Bosnia; the question is whether it should at least have been considered.

The Vance-Owen effort was a selfless mission by statesmen willing to risk their personal standing and reputation in the cause of peace. The notion of drawing new lines for new provinces is problematic, even if in

76   each a clear ethnic majority does exist. Caustic observations of Rebecca West come to mind. Writing half a century ago about the 1903 Murzsteg agreement between Turkey and the great powers, she observed:

> . . . they all passed an imbecile clause by which it was announced that as soon as Macedonia could be restored to order, the Turkish administrative districts were to be delimited anew so that they might correspond with ethnographical districts. This automatically provoked civil war of the bloodiest character. For this clause terrified the Bulgars, Serbs, and Greeks in Macedonia, who knew that there are hardly any districts which are ethnographically pure in that part of the world, and saw themselves handed over to whatever race was in the majority, by however small a figure. Each group therefore attacked both the others, and killed off as many of them as possible, with the object of reducing them to unquestionable minorities.[12]

In what was Yugoslavia, security issues will continue to loom large. The people living in areas that were the scene of mayhem will not willingly entrust their survival to foreign guarantees and control devices or to arcane constitutional procedures for their protection. They will insist on tangible and visible assurances that the force necessary for their safety is available and ready.

Beyond the immediate question of stopping the mayhem and the fighting, the hardest question is how to enforce any agreement that could be reached between the warring parties, since the Serbs continue to enjoy a clear advantage in numbers and in armaments, and how to prevent the backsliding that was a feature of past agreements made with Belgrade and its clients. I address these issues of enforcement in the final chapter.

Also worthy of mention are the serious violations by the Croatians, in 1992 and 1993, of agreements arduously negotiated by Cyrus Vance. None of the sides in the conflict in the former Yugoslavia escapes with its reputation for decency and for humanity intact.

THE KURDS

The Kurdish problem highlights a similar agenda: self-determination, the breakup and unity of states, human rights and minority rights, sovereignty, links across state frontiers, and independence. These are the issues resonating across the Balkans and the Caucasus.

After the end of hostilities in the Gulf War, the humanitarian intervention of the Allies created a new political reality. Operation Provide Comfort and the UN armed guards created a de facto autonomous area guaranteed as a "safe haven." The Kurds managed in their wartorn land to establish the machinery for self-rule and to hold elections. Their survival was secured temporarily by a fragile allied military presence in Turkey and by a "no-fly zone" barring planes of the Baghdad regime. They remain formally within the confines of the Iraqi state.

This tridimensional status—autonomy in a safe haven; foreign security umbrella; formal Iraqi sovereignty—is both unstable and temporary. The fate of the Kurds who survived the genocidal policies of the Baathist Iraqi state hangs on the power alignments in the region and on the policies of the governments in Teheran, Baghdad, Ankara, Damascus, and Riyadh. It lies also in the hands of the fickle American TV networks, whose attention wanders when their audience flags, for it does appear that American protection for the Kurds came as a result of a public outcry at their suffering and the pressure of the British allies.

The Kurdish political classes entertain few illusions about the chances of creating an independent state for the Kurds of Iraq in the immediate future. They enter-

78 tain even fewer illusions about the union of such a state with Turkish Kurdistan or with Iranian Kurdistan. They cannot struggle against the powerful tides of geopolitical concerns that have on more than one occasion led to the betrayal of their cause. The ambitions of the Iraqi Kurdish leadership are limited to those parts of Kurdistan that lie inside Iraq.

For the Kurdish people, the question is whether its physical survival is compatible with Iraqi sovereignty. In the late 1980s the Baghdad regime carried out the fully documented mass killing of Kurdish populations in the Anfal operation, as well as the systematic eradication of their villages and the destruction of their means of livelihood, their wells, and their power lines. Nevertheless, the two most influential Kurdish leaders, Masoud Barazani and Jalal Talabani, journeyed to Baghdad after Desert Storm had abated in the hope of finding a new modus vivendi with Saddam. They demonstrated in that voyage that the survival of the Kurdish nation does indeed demand the most desperate and short-lived arrangements.

The contrasting approaches to the crimes of the Serbs and of Iraq reflect the tenuous Western support for their cause. Baghdad's policies against the Kurds amounted to genocide. They were genocidal within the plain meaning of the Genocide Convention of 1948: the killing of members of a group with the intent to destroy in whole or in part a national or ethnic group as such. Yet, even as the Security Council decided to establish a war crimes tribunal for Yugoslavia, the Iraqi war criminals remain unindicted, and no tribunal is being established for their trial.

The international community must consider whether the Kurds can be expected to settle for a future within a state guilty of the most heinous crimes against them. But it also will have to weigh the consequences of a policy leading to the dismemberment of Iraq. Many believe that the breakup of the Iraqi state would enhance the paramountcy of Iranian power in the Mesopotamian region and in the Persian Gulf area. Moreover, the concerns of Turkey about potential secessionist demands by its Kurds are certain to be respected.

The temporary rescue of the Kurds from the savagery of Saddam's forces has created a situation (the stationing of American and other forces in Turkey and the overflight of Iraq by F-16s) that can neither continue for long nor come to an end, for it would signify the abandonment of the Kurds yet once again. Efforts to reconstitute Kurdish autonomy within the Iraqi state, as originally contemplated in the treaty of Lausanne, are unlikely to succeed with a regime like Baghdad's.

Autonomy in a state without democracy has scant practical meaning. Time and time again the Kurds lived to learn that juridical autonomy means little in a country in which power alone rules and whose traditions of government remain close to those of Baghdad's medieval Mongol conquerors.

The future of the Kurds highlights the problem of a nation confronting its own hostile state. It cries out for a solution involving a halfway house between full conventional independence and traditional juridical autonomy. But in the case of the Kurds, a solution is required that would shelter them from the presence of Saddam's forces and of his secret police. Any formula that affirms the continuing formal territorial integrity of Iraq must preclude the physical presence of Baghdad's men in Kurdistan, except conceivably in the framework of mixed instrumentalities. Various shared endeavors of an

80 economic character involving the oil industry, the pipelines, and agriculture would be imaginable.

The international status of the Kurds could be safeguarded, to a point, by giving the Kurds broader access to international agencies. Such access could be limited to issues that directly affect their interests. Kurdish representatives have already appeared before bodies of the U.S. Congress. They could be given similar access to UN organs dealing with items of direct interest to them—for example, hearings by the Commission on Human Rights; by the Economic and Social Council and its subsidiary organs; and, more significantly, by the Security Council. Their participation in the proceedings of international organizations and of the U.S. Congress can encourage a measure of continuing international concern once their plight has been forgotten again and the focus of attention has shifted elsewhere.

The security of the Kurdish people will continue to depend on their ability to defend themselves and on the presence of an international aerial umbrella that will eventually be based further in the Mediterranean. Whether a solution of this character is acceptable will depend in part on the wisdom of the Kurdish leadership and on its readiness to disavow political claims to Kurdish areas in the neighboring states. It will require a kind of "Macedonian" declaration, repudiating any claim to the territory and provinces of Turkey, Iran, and Syria.

In the present correlation of forces in their region, the Kurds can at best hope for an internationally protected, internationally guaranteed, and internationally recognized autonomy within nominal Iraqi sovereignty. The horrors of the past and the fears of the future militate for a solution along territorial lines leading to the end of Iraqi presence of non-Kurdish forces in their territory. To obtain this, the Kurds will have to demonstrate their effective control of Iraqi Kurdistan. Caught between Baghdad and Ankara, the Kurds have little choice but to collaborate with Turkey and help restrain the violence of the Kurdish PKK rebels in Turkey.

In practical terms, the dependence of the Kurds of northern Iraq on the goodwill of the government in Ankara has deepened. The survival of their entity in northern Iraq hangs on a supply route from Turkey. Neither the Allied presence nor the Kurds' economic survival is possible without the support of the Turkish government. Although the relative liberalization in Turkish policies toward Turkey's Kurdish minority was a short-lived affair, the Kurdish leaders in northern Iraq have looked for closer ties to Turkey. They have been careful not to fan the enmity of the Syrian and Iranian regimes. All the while, Turkey's operations against the PKK guerrillas continue relentlessly, and the battle for the minds of the 10 million Turkish Kurds is far from decided. In the summer of 1992 the PKK was reportedly getting some help from Iran even as its leader remained in Damascus. The extent of Syrian support for its activities remains unclear, despite Hafez el Asad's commitments to close the PKK training in Lebanon's Bekaa Valley and his assurances that the PKK is no longer in Syrian territory. The visit of Prime Minister Demirel of Turkey to Damascus in January 1993 was meant, among other things, to have Syria end the asylum granted to the PKK leader.

A gradual shift in opinion about the value of the integrity of Iraq as a unitary state is under way in the West. Such a state, with its history of crimes against the Kurds in the north and against the Shi'as in the south, cannot constitute a unified or firm bulwark against the

82 mounting power of Iran. To retain its unity, Iraq must be ruled either by a brutal regime in Baghdad, which would threaten the whole region, or by a weak federal government that would allow the north and the south to pursue their separate paths. In either case, there will be no meaningful counterweight to Iran. Increasing dismay in the West over the survival of Saddam's regime and increasing concern in the Arabian peninsula over its implications have weakened support for the idea of a strong government in Baghdad.

Some analysts conclude that the ascendancy of the Iranians can be checked only if Turkey can assert its influence over the Iraqi Kurdish provinces of Kirkuk and Mosul. This is an abhorrent prospect for the conservative Arab states that freed themselves from the Ottoman yoke only seven decades ago. But left to face Iranian might without the comfort of a serious buffer to their north, the Saudis and Gulf Arabs may in the end recognize that the extension of Turkey's influence—not sovereignty—into northern Iraq can provide some of the protection they crave.

None of these developments would require boundary changes. The formal integrity of the Iraqi state can be reconciled with an autonomous Kurdish province enjoying close ties to Turkey.

In early 1993 the foreign ministers of Turkey, Iran, and Syria met in Damascus to reassert their firm opposition to the establishment of a Kurdish state in northern Iraq. Such a state, they said, would constitute a threat to the integrity of the three countries. On the other hand, the Turkish foreign minister reportedly supported any formula, including a federal formula, the Kurds chose, provided it was within the framework of a unified Iraq. In early 1993 the precarious balance safeguarding the

Kurdish entity endures. But its future, like the future of the entire area, remains darkened by prospects of violence and war.

ARMENIA AND AZERBAIJAN

In this conflict, there is a formal quasi-symmetry between the two sides in regard to two enclaves: Nagorno-Karabakh, an Armenian-dominated enclave within Azerbaijan; and the autonomous republic of Nakhichevan, an Azerbaijani enclave with a small Shi'ite population sandwiched between Armenia, Turkey, and Iran. The present status of the two regions was settled in the Treaty of Moscow of 1921. Nakhichevan has been part of Azerbaijan since 1924.

The conflict over Nagorno-Karabakh began before the dissolution of the Soviet Union. In January 1992 the majority Armenians in the enclave declared independence after the collapse of the Soviet Union. Armenian President Levon Ter Petrosyan withheld recognition, a recognition that would further complicate a resolution of the conflict. The Armenian government maintains that it extends humanitarian aid only to the Armenians in the enclave. In 1992 the Armenians succeeded in establishing a corridor to the enclave. The fighting between the two sides threatened to get completely out of hand.

Armenia and Russia are parties to the collective security pact of the CIS. Azerbaijan has not joined the CIS, and Armenia is surrounded by non-CIS states (Turkey, Iran, Georgia, and Azerbaijan). Armenia was reported to have appealed to members of the pact for assistance after Azerbaijani troops penetrated an Arme-

84   nian district beyond Lake Levan. Russian forces were reportedly fighting alongside the Armenians in both enclaves.

Armenia is in a dire economic situation, which worsened when civil strife in Georgia closed off a crucial gas pipeline; in January 1993 Georgian engineers were still trying to set up an emergency gas supply pipeline. In November 1992 the hereditary enemy, Turkey, undertook to sell electricity to energy-starved Armenia. However, under pressure from nationalists at home, Ankara has delayed implementing the agreement. Turkey's ambivalence is also expressed in the encouragement given to the Azerbaijani inhabitants of Nakhichevan, who are linked to Turkey by a newly widened bridge. A 20-kilometer common border runs between Turkey and Nakhichevan.

The dangers of foreign intervention in this conflict are all too apparent; in 1992 Russian Defense Minister Marshal Shaposhnikov went so far as to suggest that Turkish intervention on the side of the Azerbaijanis could trigger a third world war. In February 1993 the Azerbaijani defense minister accused a Russian regiment of helping the Armenians in an early winter offensive in the enclave. In August 1992 President Nursultan Nazarbayev of Kazakhstan tried to broker an agreement to end the fighting. Earlier attempts by Iran and by the CSCE to mediate the conflict failed. Iran is concerned that the upheavals in the Caucasus can arouse its own Azerbaijani population. In early 1993 a sixth attempt was under way for a CSCE peace conference on Nagorno-Karabakh. In February 1993 President Eduard Shevardnadze of Georgia introduced a note of optimism, asserting that the leaders of the two sides in the

Armenian-Azerbaijani conflict have the political will to settle.

Armenia and Azerbaijan will have to look for ways to reconcile the claims of the inhabitants of the two enclaves and the integrity of their two countries. A sketch of what such arrangement could look like is perhaps premature; it is certainly presumptuous. Formulas similar to those tried in Cyprus, which remain to be tried in the Balkans, might have relevance to the Caucasus. The alternative is partition along ethnic lines, the establishment of a new border, and the painful transfer of populations that these would require.

Under a hypothetical example, the attributes of Azerbaijani and of Armenian sovereignty would be disassembled and redistributed. This would require the superimposition of national home regimes—over and in addition to the existing Armenian and Azerbaijani states. For example, and this is an example only, the Armenian enclave of Nagorno-Karabakh might, under a national home regime, form part of an internationally recognized Armenian national home in an Azerbaijani state. This would grant it more than the autonomy envisaged by the Gorbachev plan. A national home regime would allow the Armenians in Nagorno-Karabakh to associate their local institutions and agencies with those of Armenia itself. They might also be allowed to participate in the political life of Armenia. Nagorno-Karabakh would thus formally remain part of Azerbaijan, albeit as part of the Armenian National Home with Armenian rights guaranteed and secured by a powerful neighbor. The institutions of the CIS, such as they may be, could be available to share selected government powers with the Azerbaijanis and with the Armenians in disputed areas. Troublesome issues of land use

86 and title could be handled by municipal governments rather than by symbolically salient state agencies. Some land use matters could also be assigned to special mixed authorities responsible for the environment and for natural resources. Mixed tribunals or third-party agencies, such as those of the CIS, could handle matters of criminal jurisdiction involving disputes in the enclaves between Armenians and Azerbaijanis. The territorial component in conflicts among nations cannot be ignored. At bottom, the right to dispose of land, especially of public lands, must be addressed in a manner that is both simple and comprehensible.

★　★　★

The ethnic conflicts discussed above are intended to suggest that a new approach can help structure solutions other than those usually considered for their resolution. Moreover, the vision of possible outcomes that all sides could live with can contribute to the process that makes conflicts ripe for settlement.

The United States is in need of a principled policy for addressing the conflicts that involve claims for self-determination and for secession. The traditional Wilsonian commitment to self-determination offers an uncertain guide at best. The idealistic and moralistic strain in American opinion cannot be neglected with impunity. A failure to rescue victims of the Bosnian war from genocide, from the horrors of concentration camps, and from mass rapes, which the American people can see nightly on their television screens, could have a profound unsettling effect on public opinion. American intervention in areas such as the Gulf—in which vital American interests are directly at stake—could be jeopardized by popular disenchantment with a government willing to shed blood for oil, but not for people.

The United States can help bring about inevitable changes in the international order by considering solutions to ethnic strife that do not necessarily require formal territorial changes. Such a policy can identify the United States as an ally of nations striving for self-determination without pitting this country against states determined to defend their territorial integrity. The adoption of a states-plus-nations policy would keep Washington on high moral ground. The Yugoslavian wars have demonstrated that ethnic cleansing is not a policy that the United States can countenance. The Security Council has formally condemned that strategy. What the Irish problem, the Cyprus problem, the Kurdish question, and the killings in the Caucasus have in common is the need for an approach breaking new ground and for wider conceptual horizons. They call for the conscious enlargement of the international state system and for the inclusion of a system of nations.

CHAPTER 4

Intervention in Foreign Conflicts

The issue of intervention in foreign conflicts—whether ethnic or otherwise—is obscured by a tangle of legal doctrines and intense ideological expectations. The principle of nonintervention, doctrines of collective intervention and multilateralism, collective self-defense, collective security, and humanitarian intervention, arguments about the scope of authority of the Security Council and of regional organizations—these are all snagged in a web of legal and policy considerations. The Gulf War threw a harsh light on these issues; the lessons of the war have a bearing on ethnic conflicts, as well as on the broader aspects of multilateralism.

The issues involved in collective intervention in civil wars are not fundamentally different from those raised in international conflicts, although the legal norms that govern them are profoundly dissimilar. Ethnic warfare poses certain immediate challenges that are easy to identify: to prevent a spread of the conflict, to promote a cease-fire between the parties, to deliver humanitarian assistance, to press for an end to violations of humanitarian law, and to help negotiations for a settlement. The trouble is that some of these steps may require the use of armed force in circumstances that could lead to a widening war with the participation of foreign armies. Then the question arises whether collective intervention should take place at all, what it can achieve, and at what cost.

The juridical divide between international conflicts and domestic strife must be viewed with circumspection. The wisdom of broad normative statements indiscriminately governing all types of civil wars remains to be established. The characterization of a conflict as "domestic" or as "international" is a question that has long vexed jurists. States can shift the juridical divide between these two categories with ease when ethnic groups declare independence. The act of recognition by a foreign state transforms the legal nature of a conflict; yet, under prevailing international practice, recognition is granted or withheld at the discretion of foreign governments. Legal categories that are that susceptible to the political will of states should be appraised in political terms; they fail the basic test of a legal norm, which is to impose a principled restraint on untrammeled discretion. Thus, for example, the conflict between Serbs and Croats over the future of Yugoslavia was "transformed" from civil strife into a conflict between states once the EC, at the insistence of Germany, recognized Croatian and Slovenian independence. The unraveling of Yugoslavia led to the independence of Bosnia-Herzegovina and to the bitter war that followed. Serbia claimed that the JNA (Yugoslav National Army) was withdrawn from Bosnia once it ceased to form part of Yugoslavia, that the Bosnian Serbs rose against the Bosnian government in Sarajevo, and that the ensuing war was not Belgrade's responsibility. The United States recognized Bosnia in 1992; from that point on,

90   the juridical character of Serbia's assistance to the Serbian rebels in Bosnia changed.

A majority of states—guardians of sovereignty—hold that legal considerations can and should condition the collective response to ethnic wars and to massacres within a country. They insist that state consent is an absolute prerequisite for the presence of outside forces in their realm. They adhere to the principle of nonintervention even in the face of unspeakable human tragedies, ever fearful of allowing a precedent for outside intervention that could one day be invoked against them. Its sustained application in the Horn of Africa, in Ethiopia, and in the Sudan, where famine has claimed the lives of hundreds of thousands in the past decade, could bring the whole international legal order into disrepute. States that raise this principle, to object to intervention in the face of massive human suffering, say all we need to know about their own character. After delicate negotiations, in 1991 the General Assembly finally adopted a precedent-shattering resolution on the guiding principles for humanitarian assistance.[1]

It is safe to assume that legal considerations weigh less heavily with policymakers, who must determine whether to join the fray, than with the professional legal community. Evidently, those who decide not to intervene, to sit it out and to let events on the ground unfold, find comfort in legal doctrines that inhibit intervention.

International lawyers are broadly split between statists, who hold that the integrity of the state system should be upheld if anarchy is to be avoided, and interventionists. The statists remain faithful to the language and concepts of article 2.7 of the UN Charter, which prohibits intervention in matters that are "essentially" within the domestic jurisdiction of states. The interventionists, on the other hand, would give priority to a widening agenda of higher concerns. This agenda includes assistance to populations in the event of natural disasters, armed conflicts, and grave threats to the environment; the prevention of genocide; and the prevention of the proliferation of weapons of mass destruction.

In the view of the statist school of international lawyers, the state system is not all that bad. Classical international law restricts the rights of states to act within the territory of other states. The difference between the statist and interventionist approaches lies in the manner in which they balance the principle of nonintervention against other interests. Louis Henkin wrote only a few years ago, "Surely, the law cannot warrant any state's intervening by force against the political independence and territorial integrity of another on the ground that human rights are being violated, as indeed they are everywhere." He also argued that "clearly, it was the original intent of the Charter to forbid the use of force even to promote human rights or to install authentic democracy. Nothing has happened to justify deviation from that commitment."[2] Fidelity to the principle of nonintervention is designed to buttress state sovereignty. The value of an organized state is not to be belittled: the absence of governmental authority makes apocalyptic anarchy possible, as events in Somalia, which can illustrate the darkest pages of Hobbes's *Leviathan*, have demonstrated.

During the Cold War, intervention in the internal affairs of states posed risks of conflict escalation that could have embroiled the superpowers themselves. The norms prohibiting intervention restrained conduct that could have entangled the United States and the Soviet Union in armed conflict. While these norms also protected the sovereignty of weaker members of the international community, their vitality was derived from superpower relations. With the end of the Cold War, a key rationale for the prohibition of intervention has also come to an end. That is not to say that the vigor of this principle is exhausted or that the protection of the independence of weaker states is no longer warranted. In the UN at least, this principle retains its vitality as a tool for the protection of the weaker states from the great powers.

COLLECTIVE SECURITY AND COLLECTIVE INTERVENTION

With public attention riveted on Yugoslavia, the Kurds, the Caucasus, and Somalia, it is good to recall that civil wars are not triggered by ethnic or by religious passions alone. The great civil wars of the 20th century—in Russia, in Spain, and in China—were waged for other stakes; they involved neither secession nor ethnic separation. The observations that follow, are however, limited to collective intervention in ethnic conflicts.

The practice of the Security Council establishes that threats to international peace can arise within states as well as among them; the Council has affirmed its competence to act in both sets of circumstances. When a "situation" or a "dispute" between states threatens international peace, collective security becomes an issue. Collective security and collective intervention are different concepts. Collective security involves a multilateral response to an illegal act, to the use of force in violation of the UN Charter, or to an armed attack against a state protected by a defense treaty. Collective intervention is a broader, less-legalistic concept; it includes responses to illegal acts, but embraces also actions taken for humanitarian purposes or for reasons of public policy.

The central issue is whether the survival of threatened nations and peoples that have no state of their own should come within the ambit of collective security doctrines or whether the protection assured by this doctrine should be extended to sovereign states only.

Classical international law does not address the right of nations—as distinct from states—to defend themselves against massacres or against acts of terror. Under international law, Iraq's treatment of the Kurds would not have been a matter of international concern except to the extent that treaty provisions to which Iraq is a party warrant the diplomatic involvement of other states.

The authority of the Security Council to permit collective intervention for the protection of populations facing grievous domestic threats is evolving. Thus, the Council authorized Operation Restore Hope in Somalia in a situation of total anarchy after governmental power had broken down. Even Zimbabwe, a state that had long jealously defended the principle of nonintervention, concurred with the authorization.

International practice began to evolve after the Gulf War, when the Kurds of Iraq rose against the Baghdad regime, which then fought back with its customary savagery. The Kurds fled to the snow-covered mountains, to Turkey, and to Iran in an exodus that took many thousands of lives. On April 17, 1991, the United States, Britain, and France sent forces to northern Iraq, without seeking the consent of the Baghdad government, to create a safe haven for the Kurds. Twelve days

94   earlier the Security Council had adopted resolution 688, which demanded that Iraq end the repression of its civilian population, and which insisted further that Iraq allow immediate access to its territory by international humanitarian organizations. Allied officials maintained that the purpose of Operation Provide Comfort was humanitarian and not political, and that it was authorized by the Security Council. Secretary-General Javier Pérez de Cuéllar disagreed. He maintained that the Allied military presence on Iraqi territory required either the consent of the Iraqi government or the express authorization of the Council. The secretary-general upheld a strict statist view, in contrast to the Allies, who intervened in Iraq over the objections of its government and without specific Council authority.

The contrast between the statist and the interventionist approaches was reflected in the Security Council debate. China and India insisted that the principle of nonintervention in internal affairs be protected. On April 18 the Baghdad government signed a Memorandum of Understanding (MOU) that permitted the deployment in Iraq of UN "guards" and the establishment of UN Humanitarian Centers. This MOU applied to all of Iraq's territory and included areas in the south of the country where the Shi'ite rebellion was continuing. Iraq signed the MOU under the pressure of Allied military action that had begun a day earlier. In the summer of 1992 the Allies took action to establish another safe haven in the south, for the protection of the Shi'ites. The United States, Britain, and France decreed a second no-fly zone, south of the 34th parallel, from which all aircraft of the Baghdad government were barred.

The safe haven created for the Kurds in northern Iraq and the no-fly zone established to protect the

Shi'ites in the south constitute a departure from traditional practices, even though they are firmly grounded
in the terms of the Council's resolution that established a
cease-fire regime for Iraq. In January 1993, during the
last days of the Bush presidency, the Baghdad government challenged the legality of the no-fly zones and
began to resist their enforcement, arguing that the Security Council had not specifically sanctioned them. Iraqi
military action against coalition aircraft led to the
bombing of Iraqi targets by U.S. forces both inside and
outside the two zones. France, a coalition member, ob-
jected that the bombing of targets in the Baghdad area
exceeded the authority granted by Security Council
resolutions.

The events in Iraqi Kurdistan and in Bosnia have
revived the debate over the legitimacy of the use of force
to assist civilian populations and to promote human
rights. But this debate is essentially of an academic
nature, since in practice, when the Security Council is
intent on acting, it invokes its powers under chapter 7
of the Charter. This step puts an end to all juridical
debates. The Security Council has demonstrated that it
is the sole judge of the circumstances that warrant recourse
to chapter 7. Under the Charter, the five permanent
Council members, plus five nonpermanent members,
have the supreme juridical authority in the Council to
act as they see fit. No challenges to this authority have
been entertained as yet.

The Charter has not created a system of checks and
balances on the powers of the Council. Hence, the
Council can authorize the use of force to promote human rights when, at its discretion, it chooses to act
under chapter 7. The framers of the Charter decided that
each UN organ would determine its own authority

96   under the Charter. They rejected the suggestion that the International Court of Justice sit in review. Dissenting states have no persuasive juridical recourse against the Council; they are bound by article 25 of the Charter to carry out its decisions, and they are committed under article 103 to give their obligations under the Charter priority over any other treaty obligation. For example, the Council decided to impose universal mandatory commercial and diplomatic sanctions on Libya. This action was aimed at securing compliance with the Council's resolution demanding that the Libyan government surrender two nationals allegedly involved in the Pan Am Lockerbie bombing.

In *Libya v. U.S.*, the World Court rebuffed a challenge to the Council's decision to impose sanctions. This decision led to the question whether the Court had abdicated the power to review Council resolutions or whether it had merely failed to affirm its authority to do so. Some of the opinions rendered in the case lend themselves to a reading affirming the power of review. An analogy was even drawn between the Court's decision in *Libya v. U.S.* and *Marbury v. Madison*, in which Chief Justice Marshall affirmed the authority of the Supreme Court of the United States to review the constitutionality of acts of Congress.[3] Such comparisons make sense only if it can be argued that UN members are committed to create a more perfect union of a federal character among themselves. Efforts to transpose American constitutional doctrines to the inhospitable terrain of international adjudication should be made with care; the Court is no doubt acutely aware that it possesses neither the power of the purse nor that of the sword. The Council, on the other hand, can scarcely ignore that effective multilateral action often requires the concurrence of states that are not members. Thus the economic sanctions imposed on Iraq failed to prevent the reconstruction of plants and facilities damaged during the war, which is helped by continuing trade across the borders of Jordan, Turkey, and Iraq.

The invasion of Kuwait and the war in Yugoslavia bear eloquent witness to what Western nations will do when their interests are menaced and to what they will *not* do when they do not feel directly threatened. The crises in the Gulf and in the Balkans since 1990 have tested the proposition that with the collapse of the Soviet Union, the permanent five Security Council members can use the Council to maintain international peace and security. The high expectations born of the resolute stand against Saddam's invasion of Kuwait have already largely dissipated. Doubts arise again about the very enterprise of collective security. Writing in early 1991, Henry Kissinger argued that the basic premises of collective security do not apply in the international community as we know it—that, in other words, it is conceptually flawed.[4] This is a world of players with different pasts, with different interests, and with different traditions. It is highly unrealistic to expect that they would be willing to subordinate pressing national interests to the need to uphold international law or to enforce peace in regions they can afford to ignore. The recent historical record has borne him out. In 1992 the great powers were not willing to use force to impose a ceasefire in Yugoslavia. The public debate in America and in Western Europe about the wisdom of providing military protection for humanitarian assistance tended to obscure the fact that no country was willing to risk sending its soldiers to force an end to the conflict. For over a year and a half, the powers did nothing in a

98　situation that the Council itself characterized as a threat to international peace, except to impose blatantly ineffective economic sanctions on Serbia.

MULTILATERALISM IN THE GULF WAR

As the Gulf War demonstrated, the collective security doctrine is of great value to the United States. It is sobering to examine how the Security Council was used during the war, and to contrast its actions then with its response to the situation in the former Yugoslavia. The Gulf War briefly heightened expectations that a new era of collective security was about to begin. This would be an age in which, in the words of President Bush, "the rule of law . . . governs the conduct of nations."[5] Security Council resolution 678, which authorized the use of force to liberate Kuwait, came close to realizing this ideal. Or so it appeared. But some observers saw it differently. The columnist Charles Krauthammer wrote, "Collective security? In the Gulf, without the United States leading and prodding, bribing and blackmailing, no one would have stirred. . . . There is a sharp distinction to be drawn between real and apparent multilateralism. . . . What we have today is pseudomultilateralism." The danger, in his view, was that American political leaders might believe their own "pretense."[6]

The Gulf War may have been atypical in more ways than one. Many of the conflicts that now confront the world are of a totally different character. They do not necessarily involve an attack across accepted international boundaries. A more central concern of the world community is to stifle internal hostilities that can lead to large refugee migrations and provoke the intervention of neighboring states.

The preservation worldwide of minimal standards of civilization could well become part of a revised concept of the national interest, either as a requirement of a peaceful world or for its own sake as an absolute value. In any event, with the Cold War at an end, it is difficult to believe that either the Congress or the American people would support military operations overseas—either unilateral or multilateral—that are unrelated to a direct threat to "vital American interests"; this concept cannot be enlarged at will to legitimize the use of force.

Important segments of American opinion question the right of the United States to use force unilaterally—except in clear-cut cases of self-defense—without the authorization of the international community and without the approval of the Congress. The War Powers Resolution is still on the books. The president needs congressional authority to wage war, whether or not he concedes the constitutionality of that legislation.[7]

The link between international authorization for the use of force and congressional approval became apparent in the weeks preceding Operation Desert Storm. President Bush used the principles of collective security to great effect to overcome the stigma attached to the unilateral American intervention in Vietnam. Security Council resolution 678 legitimized in the eyes of Americans the use of force by the United States. This is one of the main lessons drawn from the congressional debate that preceded the Gulf War. Resolution 678 helped sway hesitant votes in the Congress. The fact that, according to credible reports, the United States had to buy at least one of the votes in the Security Council made no difference. The Congress was not

100   concerned to inquire which Security Council members authorized the use of force, or why. It accepted the Council's decision without question.

Although the United States resorted to the Council to legitimize the military campaign against Iraq and to buttress its fragile coalition with the Arab states, the decision to use force was essentially an American one. The Council had no say about the conduct of the military operations. The UN Military Staff Committee was not involved.

To be sure, initially, the president was ready to come to the assistance of Kuwait even without the backing of the Council, and even though the United States had no mutual defense treaty with Kuwait. The United States was ready to take military action on the basis of article 51 of the Charter, which reaffirms the inherent right of states to "collective" self-defense. Later, the president decided to act through the Security Council. The reasons that led him to do so are not all known yet.[8]

Two decisions had to be made: the decision to use force, if need be, and the decision to seek the approval of the Council for its use. The latter decision was not an obvious one. The administration knew that resort to the Council would impose constraints and reduce its freedom of action. The president's decision was fraught with risk: he would have found it difficult to launch Desert Storm if the Council, once it had decreed economic sanctions, failed to approve resolution 678. In such circumstances, the Council's rejection of the use of force would most likely have sealed the fate of the debate in this country and prevented the president from doing what he believed was necessary. He thus placed his policy at the mercy of a Chinese veto and of the votes of the Soviet Union and of France (other members would have followed), both of which until the last minute sought to strike a bargain with Saddam that the United States would not have countenanced. Resolution 678 also helped the administration obtain Japanese and German financial support for the war.

In true collective security it should make no difference who commits aggression and who the victim is. But the principles of collective security were ignored even during the Gulf War. Kissinger, among others, observed that in its finest hour, the Security Council closed its eyes to that principle when Israel was attacked. The Council failed even to take note of the Iraqi missile attacks on Israeli towns so as not to undermine the U.S.-led coalition. Kissinger's observation may strike one as a formalistic quibble at a time when Israel's sworn adversary was itself under assault. Tactically, the Council's silence made eminent sense, but the implications of this omission are sobering, for they confirm yet again that the Council is governed less by the commitment to respond to unprovoked aggression than by the politics of the situation.[9]

COLLECTIVE INTERVENTION AND SELF-DEFENSE

The connection between the unilateral use of force in self-defense and the use of force formally authorized by the Security Council remains of cardinal importance. International law does not prohibit the unilateral use of force by states in all circumstances. The principles of customary international law do not require the Security Council to approve all uses of force. They permit the unilateral and the collective use of force in self-defense against armed attacks and, some would argue, against

102   acts of aggression—like maritime blockades and other "acts of war"—that fall short of armed attacks. Anticipatory self-defense, however, is another matter, even if it might be condoned in exceptional emergency situations. Its legality has been widely challenged.

Under article 51 of the Charter, the use of force in self-defense is permitted *until* the Security Council has taken the measures necessary to preserve international peace and security. Actions taken in self-defense, whether individual or collective, require no international authorization *until* the Security Council has taken the measures necessary to maintain international peace and security.[10] Military actions taken in self-defense are legitimate even without the endorsement of the Security Council. The right of self-defense is an *inherent* right; it is not conferred by the Charter of the UN or by any other international treaty. It can be exercised freely, within the limits set by international law—limits dictated by considerations of necessity and proportionality—until the Security Council has taken the "measures necessary." Hence, the right of self-defense legitimizes the use of force "if an armed attack occurs" without the *prior* authorization of any international agency.

The United States may yet again be driven to invoke the doctrine of collective self-defense should one of its allies be the victim of an act of aggression *and* should the Security Council fail to take action by reason of a veto or otherwise. It may be a miscalculation to assume that Russia—staking out an independent Gaullist-like foreign policy—has permanently forsworn its use of the veto. China may likewise be led to cast its veto to block resolutions under chapter 7 of the Charter. The end of the Cold War does not guarantee the concurrence of the permanent members of the Security Council that is required for the adoption of resolutions on matters of substance.

While international law addresses the right of states to use force in self-defense, it is silent in regard to the right of self-defense of national and other ethnic groups that do not constitute a state. With regard to such groups, the reach of international law is limited. The law of genocide, of human rights, of minority rights, and international criminal law share a common weakness: an absence of enforcement mechanisms. The law of humanitarian intervention and the creation of safe havens is in full evolution. But the law regarding the right of ethnic groups to defend themselves still lies beyond the range of the international legal order.

Eugene Rostow has argued that the "ultimate question" presented by the Persian Gulf crisis of 1990–1991 is whether the Council can insist that no state exercise its right of individual and collective self-defense without prior Security Council permission. In the Gulf crisis, he has suggested, the Council conceived of its actions as "supplementing the programs of self-defense organized by the United States, not as supplanting them." These did not constitute "enforcement action" under articles 42–50 of the Charter, despite the use of the word "authorize" in resolution 678 that legitimized the use of force against Iraq. But could the countries that drove Iraq out of Kuwait have done so without the Council's authority? Is the "inherent" right of self-defense subordinated to Security Council permission? Does it become "dormant" when the Council puts a conflict on its agenda? Is it "subsumed by or incorporated into the global police response . . . once it begins to work?"[11]

When states are faced with armed attacks, their survival hinges on their ability to defend themselves and

104   on timely outside help. Collective intervention must be understood in the context of the right of self-defense. No substantive or procedural qualification of the right of self-defense can be lightly presumed, since it involves the very survival of states. Neither the practice of states nor the negotiating record of article 51 of the Charter suggests that the exercise of the right of self-defense can be suspended otherwise than by a formal, explicit, binding decision of the Council under chapter 7 of the Charter. No state has ever proposed to modify or to abandon this norm.

The scope of the right of self-defense remains a fundamental issue for all states in international and in domestic conflicts alike. In the controversial decision given in *Nicaragua v. United States*, the World Court purported to lay down limits on its exercise. The Court suggested that the victim of aggressive acts must in all circumstances await the occurrence of an armed attack—however grave and irreversible its effects may be—before using force in its own defense. Under this ruling, a wide array of aggressive acts do not warrant the use of force in self-defense. Even more pertinent to our discussion here, the Court would prohibit the use of force in self-defense against states that merely assist rebels in a civil war. Thus, Bosnia would presumably not be entitled to strike at JNA targets in Serbia to defend itself against the JNA's support for Bosnian rebels so long as Serbia itself commits no armed attack. Nor would other nations have the right to intervene against Serbia in order to assist Bosnia without a Security Council resolution authorizing them to do so. Actually, the Court's opinion goes even further. It would prohibit the use of force in self-defense against acts of aggression (as defined by the UN itself) that fall short of the Court's concept of an armed attack. Under the Court's opinion, a state is not entitled to strike at targets in a foreign country involved in terrorist actions against its embassies or civil aircraft, or to strike at targets in a country that is responsible for other acts of war that fall short of an armed attack. Clearly, the Court considers that not all acts of aggression constitute an armed attack. It objects to the use of force in self-defense against a wide array of acts that would have customarily been characterized as acts of war.

The opinion of the Court does not accurately reflect state practice. States will continue to rely on themselves rather than await the intervention of other powers, albeit with the imprimatur of the Security Council. Any judicial effort to articulate rules of law that, on the theory that no armed attack has been committed, requires states to expose themselves to mortal dangers or to imperil their vital interests rests on weak grounds indeed. States have never been willing to concede that international law requires them to risk the lives of citizens threatened by terrorism.

A set of grave problems involving the dissemination of chemical, bacteriological, and nuclear technology and weapons, and of the missiles that can deliver them, is likely to occupy the attention of the international community in the years to come. The debate about the legitimacy of anticipatory self-defense will acquire a new urgency. Threatened states may be tempted to act preemptively until a reliable and credible anti-ballistic missile shield can be put in place. It is doubtful that an Israeli preemptive strike on Iraqi nuclear facilities in late 1990 would have been censured as severely as the raid on the Osirak reactor ten years earlier. Collective

106   action taken in self-defense against renegade states acquiring weapons of mass destruction in violation of nonproliferation treaty may have acquired a new legitimacy in the wake of Saddam's covert nuclear efforts. This is by no means an academic subject, especially not in the Middle East. The genie of proliferation is loose. It is the more worrying since these weapons can fall into the hands of fanatical regimes that would use them in war rather than rely on them for deterrence only. Iraq's employment of chemical weapons in its war with Iran raised new fears throughout the area. Oil rich Iran's own interest in nuclear technology was confirmed by the agreements it signed in 1992 with China for the supply of nuclear reactors, presumably not needed to satisfy Iran's own energy requirements. Until quite recently, Algeria was reported to have engaged in nuclear-related work with the assistance of China. Pakistan has confirmed that it is close to having a bomb, and according to credible reports, Muammar Qaddafi is also in the market for such a weapon. North Korea's nuclear project is likewise a source of substantial concern. Israel is widely believed to have a nuclear arsenal to offset the massive conventional force superiority of its Arab enemies. This arsenal is mentioned to justify Arab acquisition of nuclear weaponry.

    In the aftermath of the Cold War, collective intervention remains possible in a narrow range of situations only. Clearly, it cannot be invoked, in the UN at least, against any veto-wielding power. It is of no avail when great powers confront one another. It can best be used against other would-be Saddams lurking in the shadows of militarized regimes in the Third World and in sanguinary regional struggles. But even then, it is of doubtful effectiveness against heavily armed regional powers, in countries with big populations and a difficult terrain. Nor is collective intervention credible against rulers who can hold regional states hostage with nuclear weapons and other weapons of mass destruction.

These considerations lead us back to the issue of the right—albeit a political and moral rather than legal right—of ethnic groups facing irreparable losses to defend themselves against policies of genocide and of ethnic cleansing. The maintenance by the Security Council of the arms embargo against the former Yugoslavia seriously impeded the Bosnian Muslim defenses against the Serb onslaught. The Serbs inherited most of the heavy weapons of the Yugoslav army. The Bosnian Muslims were at a severe disadvantage until a slow flow of arms, financed by Arab money, helped refurbish their forces in the winter of 1993. The denial of arms to the Bosnian government has a variety of rationales: from the prevention of a spread of the conflict to the security of the UN peacekeeping forces. It is fair to say that the international community obstructed the efforts of the government in Sarajevo to defend itself even as the Bosnian Muslims were exposed to genocidal attacks. The reasons for this policy were weighty, but the precedent set is ominous for small nations that can rely for their security on themselves alone.

THE UN AND REGIONAL ORGANIZATIONS

The relationship between regional organizations and the Security Council remains ambiguous. It is affected by the newfound consensus among the permanent mem-

108   bers. If the pattern of the early 1990s is any guide, the
UN may intervene in situations that in earlier times
would have been left to regional organizations to deal
with. In Central America the UN acted to end the civil
war in Salvador in an area that had traditionally been the
exclusive preserve of the OAS. The Arab League was
unable to respond to the Iraqi aggression against
Kuwait, and King Hussein's appeal to allow the Arab
states to deal with the crisis went unheeded. It was the
UN rather than the Organization of African Unity that
brought the conflict in Namibia to an end.

The question remains: Which are the international
instrumentalities with the power to *authorize* intervention in foreign lands? This is an issue of real importance.
To reiterate the obvious, the Security Council has the
clear authority to call for armed intervention in the
internal affairs of any state when it determines that a
threat to international peace is involved. The Council
has the "primary" responsibility for the maintenance of
the peace. It, and only it, has the power to authorize
enforcement action by regional organizations.

Indeed, the scope of authority of regional organizations is not specified. Chapter 8 of the UN Charter
regulates "enforcement actions" taken by "regional organizations" (this term is deliberately not defined).[12]
The recent practice of NATO is of interest. At their June
1992 meeting in Oslo, the NATO foreign ministers
decided that the Organization would support peacekeeping activities on a case-by-case basis on the specific
request of the 52-nation CSCE. The Oslo decision signaled a disposition of the United States and of its allies in
Europe to resort to NATO outside the framework of
the Security Council in peacekeeping matters. In his
1992 report, *An Agenda for Peace*, Secretary-General

Boutros-Ghali approached this subject with great caution. He said that regional agencies "in many cases possess a potential that should be utilized in serving the functions [of] preventive diplomacy, peacekeeping, peacemaking and post-conflict peace-building." He added that "should the Security Council choose specifically to authorize a regional arrangement or organization to take the lead in addressing a crisis within its region, it could serve to lend the weight of the United Nations to the validity of the regional effort." He added that these can render a great service "if their relationship with the . . . Security Council, is governed by Chapter VIII [of the Charter]."[13] The question of which organizations have the authority to permit such activities remains unclear, and so is their relationship with the Security Council. The United States, for its part, was willing to seek the authorization to intervene from organizations of a regional character. It had invoked the call of the obscure Organization of Eastern Caribbean States as a warrant for intervention in Grenada.

In the aftermath of the Gulf War, the secretary-general has again called for the Security Council to be endowed with military forces, in accordance with the special agreements contemplated in article 43. President François Mitterrand of France offered to place 1,000 men at the disposal of the Council under the direction of the Military Staff Committee. (France may, incidentally, be trying to revive indirectly the idea of a "directorate" of big powers, which President Charles de Gaulle had broached with President John F. Kennedy in discussion about the future of NATO.) A variety of proposals have emerged: for the creation of a rapid deployment force, for provisional standby peace forces, for permanent peacekeeping forces, and for forces re-

110   quired to put an end to random violence and to secure a
reasonable degree of safety for humanitarian relief effort.[14] The considerable practical and political obstacles
facing these proposals will no doubt be debated for
some time to come.

   The UN should have the means to avoid situations
in which states that make peacekeeping contingents
available can, in practice, terminate their participation
unilaterally when they see fit. The 1967 Arab-Israeli war
was precipitated in no small measure by Secretary-
General U Thant's decision to withdraw UN peacekeeping forces from the Straits of Tiran. This followed
Egyptian President Gamal Abdel Nasser's request that
they be removed to enable Egypt to blockade the straits.
Although Nasser had agreed with Secretary-General
Dag Hammarskjold that these forces would not be
withdrawn without the consent of the secretary-
general, U Thant had in practice little control over the
decision: the nations that had sent contingents wanted to
pull them out, and there was no way for the secretary-
general to keep them in position.

   In any case, the issue of the financing of multilateral
operations has not been solved. Boutros-Ghali refers to
a "chasm" between the tasks entrusted to his organization and the means provided to it. To judge by the $2
billion arrears in members' dues, the credible financing
of Security Council operations is not assured. Under
chapter 7, however, the Council may have the authority
to decide on measures of a fiscal character to finance the
actions it decides to undertake on behalf of the UN.[15]

   Several proposals have been made. These include a
levy on arms sales and a tax on international air travel—
but, significantly, not on the shipment of oil. It is difficult to believe that the Western powers are prepared—in

the short run—to endow the Council with an autonomous fiscal base and to create in this fashion another institution with the power to tax.

In *An Agenda for Peace* Boutros-Ghali laid out his program for preventive diplomacy. The question remains whether it can be extended to prevent internal disputes that lead to ethnic and religious strife and what can be done before internal crises come to a boil. The deployment of UN personnel to Macedonia in early 1993 illustrates the need for such action in a country pivotal to the maintenance of peace between Greece, Turkey, and Bulgaria.

A difficult balance must be struck between the demands of the advocates of multilateralism and the need to retain the capacity for unilateral action. Threats to a state's national interest may require the use of force without regard to Council votes. It is easy to imagine hypothetical circumstance in which this might become necessary: for example, in the event of an Iranian attack on Saudi Arabia in circumstances in which China would veto a resolution authorizing the use of force against Iran. Proposals that the United States, and the other great powers, renounce unilateral action in regional conflicts should be balanced against the need to retain the means to defend vital national interests and to come to the assistance of regional allies subjected to unlawful aggression. Thus, the United States will continue to be engaged in efforts to prevent atomic, bacteriological and chemical weapons proliferation, in the repression of terrorism, and in the preservation of the stable supply of oil at prices compatible with world economic growth; but it is hard to conceive of a situation in which Washington would neglect its vital interests because of a failure to secure Council endorsement.

112   It is also worth noting that many in the developing world perceive this new enthusiasm for peace enforcement by the Council in a somber light. The Gulf War involved military operations undertaken by nations of the rich, white, largely Christian north against a country in the poorer (though oil-rich), Islamic South. The brutality of Saddam's aggression was not in issue; there is a fear that Western powers, the United States in particular, are trying to reassert their influence everywhere under the mantle of a new world order. In early 1993 the Arab media were particularly bitter about the American raids on Iraq to enforce the no-fly zone, which stood in such sharp contrast to the failure to do anything about the no-fly zone decreed for Yugoslavia.

The evolving international order is a system of great complexity and opacity. The maintenance of peace and security in this system requires a panoply of measures and policies that go far beyond the legalistic prescription of an institutional response to illegal conduct. In the international system that is taking shape, the notion that it will be possible to keep the peace on the paradigm of domestic law enforcement remains misplaced.

THE UNITED STATES AND COLLECTIVE INTERVENTION

Economic sanctions remain the preferred enforcement instrument. The president of the United States should be given options to avoid having to commit ground forces to combat in places like Bosnia and northern Iraq. The U.S. defense establishment can be directed to stand ready for world order missions that bear little resemblance to the military operations of the past 30 years. These are missions that involve neither a Desert Storm–

style war to win a conventional victory nor a Vietnam-style stalemate fought for political ends.

Different capabilities are required for world order missions: the capability to create "hard" economic sanctions that might obviate the need to use force and the capability to come to the assistance of threatened populations. To focus on American desiderata for a moment, four principal problems require definition:

- What is the appropriate American response to armed conflicts or civil violence in situations that do not directly engage the nation's security or economic interests? (Somalia is apparently a case in point.)

- What is the appropriate response when extensive and prolonged military operations would be required to repel aggression? (Bosnia is obviously a case in point.)

- What is the appropriate response to conflicts inside large and powerful states, such as China and India, where geopolitical considerations cannot be neglected? (Religious strife between Hindus and Muslims is a case in point.)

- What is the appropriate role for NATO?

Hard Economic Sanctions

The imposition of economic sanctions that are not accompanied by measures meant to assure compliance undermines faith in the capacity of the Security Council to act meaningfully otherwise than with armed force. Enforcement measures to make economic sanctions ef-

114 fective can be made part of the sanctions regime. Sanctions can include a requirement, under article 25 of the UN Charter, that countries bordering on a targeted region permit the monitoring of those borders by international inspectors. (Saddam's regime acquired much of what it needed through the road from Jordan. The Security Council could have ordered the stationing of UN personnel on the Jordanian side of Iraq's border to stop contraband.)

Provision can also be made for the visit and search of commercial vessels not only on the high seas, but on international rivers as well. The right to visit, search, and—if need be—destroy shipping should complement the interdiction of air traffic. This right should be extended to international rivers like the Danube, which has been the main avenue for the supply of Serbia in the war. Economic sanctions imposed under chapter 7 of the Charter can include the total isolation of a country and the authority to destroy bridges, roads, and rail links on or near the borders of the targeted region.

Humanitarian Assistance

The related problem of providing assistance to threatened populations requires the development and improvement of special military capabilities. Air cover operations are essential for the protection of safe havens. (They are the pillar of Kurdish security in northern Iraq.) Contingency military and diplomatic plans are needed for basing air force units in areas in which ethnic conflicts and other disasters are developing; American air force units should have bases for operations in Yugoslav and Iraqi airspace.

The supply by air of food and of other essentials, like those distributed to the Kurds in the immediate aftermath of the war, presents problems of an operational character. The airlift during the 1949 Berlin blockade saved the city from a Soviet takeover. The supply of besieged populations by air drops is a much more complicated matter. The risks of flying low and the dangers of hostile ground fire must be balanced with the risks of high-altitude flights and imperfect drops. The difficulties faced by the Allied air forces in 1991 during the supply by air of the Kurds who fled Saddam's armies suggest that much remains to be done to improve the efficiency and accuracy of air drops; the design of guided, "smart drop" canisters might be feasible for the developers of the cruise missile. Similar drops were advocated for the supply of isolated Muslim enclaves in Bosnia. They were also advocated for Somalia, where the security of overland distribution could not be assured. The improvement of air drop techniques and the prepositioning of supplies in areas such as the Horn of Africa can be integrated with contingency planning for humanitarian purposes. (Such techniques could even have benefited the inhabitants of Dade County in Florida whose homes were devastated by Hurricane Andrew in August 1992.) The handling and the direct distribution of food aid and other emergency assistance to civilian populations in areas affected by war or by natural disaster could become a mission for the armed forces.

Humanitarian assistance can embrace the deployment of special forces to secure concentration camps and places where atrocities are committed. Special forces could open these localities to international inspection. Commandos can be tasked to apprehend persons sus-

116   pected of committing crimes under international law, such as concentration camp commanders, and hold them for eventual trial. Operations of this kind would enjoy strong popular support and help in the deterrence of the more flagrant horrors.

Financial and commercial incentives can be added to these military instruments. These should include forfeiture consequences for corporations and for individuals violating a Security Council embargo. Also, the export of embargoed goods to implausible destinations should shift the burden of proof to defendants charged with sanctions-busting. Forfeiture penalties modeled after the Racketeer Influenced and Corrupt Organization Act of 1970 can be put into effect for domestic and foreign violators over which the United States can exercise jurisdiction.

Intervention of the Media

This mode of intervention has reached such significance that it should be addressed separately. The effectiveness of international action depends in no small measure on the sustained attention of the American media. In conflicts in which material national interests—like oil—are not engaged, it has become the necessary prerequisite to collective intervention; the operation to rescue the Kurds in the spring of 1991 probably would not have begun but for the insistence of British Prime Minister John Major and the pressure of the media on President Bush. The role of the media in mobilizing popular support for American intervention in foreign crises was also evident in the period that led to Operation Provide Comfort in Somalia, although the delayed coverage of the Somali tragedy probably cost thousands of lives.

The television networks could be organized to provide less erratic coverage of foreign civil wars and disasters. Coverage of foreign conflicts has been capricious and uneven. While some conflicts dear to politicized anchormen receive excessive attention, others have been almost completely ignored. The media share a measure of moral responsibility for massacres and for starvation that go unreported. The atrocious war in southern Sudan is a case in point. Or, to take another example, in early 1993 CNN and the three big television networks virtually ignored a major battle for Kabul, Afghanistan, in which thousands of civilians were hurt; it was top of the news on the BBC world service for many days running.

The television networks and CNN could take some easy steps to discharge their responsibilities. They could, for example, establish a small advisory body of respected newsmen to alert network producers when the suffering of civilian populations in foreign wars and disasters goes unreported or neglected. It should have the authority to criticize news coverage and to urge the networks to devote more air time to situations where atrocities occur. The lives of millions of people in remote lands depend on the air time the networks are willing to devote to their plight. Intervention by television is an instrument of considerable potency and should be used responsibly. The moral and political responsibility of the news network in the coverage of foreign conflicts is a subject that calls for more attention by those concerned with ethics in world affairs.

The Use of Force

During his last weeks in office, President Bush attempted to spell out when the use of force might be

118   warranted.[16] He warned that force might not always be
the best way to protect a national interest that qualifies
as important; on the other hand, he said, force may be
warranted to protect an interest that, as in the case of
Somalia, is less than vital. It can be a useful complement
to diplomacy or, if need be, a temporary alternative. He
started a debate that, significantly, is *not* conducted in
terms of what the UN Charter authorizes or prohibits;
he was concerned that principle not displace prudence.
The position of President Bush was echoed in January
1993 during the confirmation hearings of Secretary of
State Warren Christopher. He took pains to assert that
the "discreet and careful" use of force may be required
to maintain the United States as a world power.

The use of force for the maintenance of peace requires difficult decisions. It requires a painstaking
avoidance of civilian targets and a choice of objectives
that should not unduly imperil the health and physical
safety of ordinary inhabitants. Two very different kinds
of military intervention must be distinguished. One
kind involves the dispatch of ground forces for combat
duties to block and roll back an invading army. The
other involves the use of air power. The United States is
committed not to repeat the errors of the Vietnam War;
the armed forces are determined not to be caught in a
quagmire in which they cannot fight for a complete
military victory. Under the so-called Weinberger doctrine, the United States must enjoy overwhelming,
massive advantage to assure complete victory in as short
a period of time as possible, to minimize American
casualties. The president should be able to extricate
American forces without difficulty.

In a country like Yugoslavia, the conditions for
such a military operation cannot be met; the terrain, the

adversary, and the politics preclude a quick victory on the model of Desert Storm. Hence the fear of entanglement, amplified by awareness of the woes of the German occupant during the Second World War.

The choice between two main options—the use of massive force on the ground (troops) and punitive air strikes—is easily misunderstood. The persistent, unremitting targeting of the political command and control apparatus of an aggressor and of his communication links must be distinguished from sporadic raids having the character of reprisals. Air power can be used for mere retaliation, but it can also convince an aggressor that the price of aggression is too high and that the price will have to be paid for too long. What air power cannot achieve by brute force, it can attain by persistence:

Air Power to Change a Regime. In the former Yugoslavia, for example, air operations could have targeted the Serb leadership and command and control centers. These could be exposed to sustained, uninterrupted pain. A promise of long-lasting, routine misery might have some effect when destined to continue until a regime change and until guilty leaders are brought to justice. This could be complemented, for example, by the destruction of Danube bridges, highway and railroad overpasses, power stations, television and radio facilities, and phone exchanges. Bombing that does not threaten the health and physical safety of the population at large could be carried out for months. It would, however, require the removal of UN peacekeeping forces, which might be targeted in two-way fire by the belligerents. While the deployment of peacekeeping forces should not impede collective intervention, the

120   peacekeeping forces in Bosnia did in fact impose constraints on collective intervention. Secretary Christopher confirmed that the presence of UN forces in Bosnia was one of the considerations inhibiting American action to enforce a no-fly zone and to rearm the Bosnian side. The Gulf War and the bombing of Iraq did not demonstrate that air power cannot procure a regime change. Neither Desert Storm nor the economic sanctions were aimed at the removal of Saddam. His removal was not part of the formal UN mandate for the liberation of Kuwait. All military operations were halted before the government in Baghdad could be changed. Air power, combined with the indictment of war criminals in the leadership, should drive home the notion that there would be no escape for the guilty.

Air Power to Punish an Aggressor. The use of air power to "punish" an aggressor is rarely effective. The limited air raids on Iraq in January 1993, when Saddam chose to challenge the no-fly zones, neither punished the regime nor weakened it. On the contrary, it exposed the fault lines in the coalition. The sporadic use of air power to punish an aggressor should not be confused with sustained raids to get rid of an aggressive regime. Its features and its policy objectives are fundamentally different. Raids to punish an aggressor can only serve other policy ends: to affirm a commitment to oppose the guilty party or to keep public attention focused on the wrongdoer.

    Collective intervention should be guided by political rather than by formal juridical objectives, with a clear differentiation between strategies to punish an aggressor, strategies to contain or to repel aggression, and strategies to overturn aggressive regimes. These are distinct objectives that require distinct strategies.

The Security Council has the authority to focus on the threat to international peace inherent in certain regimes and types of conduct, and not merely on the acts of aggression that have to be reversed. The problem with Desert Storm lay in the declared war aims. President Bush announced that the conquest of Kuwait "shall not stand." He did not proclaim that the Iraqi regime shall not remain in power, though he did call for the removal of Saddam by the Iraqi people. The Council could have decided that air operations against Saddam's regime should continue, albeit on a narrower range of targets, until his removal was assured. To achieve this, there was no need to march on to Baghdad. The integrity of the Iraqi state might have been better safeguarded by driving Saddam out than by allowing him to remain in power.

CHAPTER 5

Conclusion

The response to ethnic conflicts should rest on three pillars: a diplomatic pillar, an enforcement pillar, and a humanitarian pillar. On the diplomatic side, we have looked at a new set of concepts—the states-plus-nations approach.[1] On the enforcement side, we have looked at a leadership-busting strategy, a vigorous, credible collective enforcement strategy that does *not* require the deployment of American ground forces overseas. On the humanitarian side, aid to the victims of conflict should be dispensed in a manner that would neither widen the war nor inhibit necessary enforcement measures.

A fourth pillar should be carefully preserved: a pillar of prudence and of pragmatism. American opinion is not well attuned to understand the loathing and histories that feed remote hatreds in foreign lands. The past is indeed prologue, but in many places it is a prologue to further wars and atrocities. No two conflicts are alike, and no two histories resemble each other. Hence, the adoption of set policies and boilerplate normative responses to ethnic conflicts would be a menace in itself. A most careful analysis is needed in every case. The United States does not aspire to be involved in every conflict in every remote land. This nation has neither the means nor the ambition to shoulder such responsibilities. American opinion will not support it.

When this book was in its first draft, in early 1992, the question of the entitlement of ethnic minorities to collective international protection from genocide was still very much an open question. A year later, with the images of the Bosnian war before us, this principle has made great strides toward being accepted as a guide for American policy. But its very nobility and the strength of its appeal present also the greatest difficulty. Unchecked by considerations of prudence and the calculus of American capabilities, this principle could yet drive the United States, with inadequate resources, into hopelessly complex wars. None of this is meant to dampen the entirely appropriate response—in human terms and in terms of American values—to atrocities. In a world in which America has a role to play, and in which it hopes to be morally at peace with itself, there are certain horrors that it must repress.

The repression of genocide cannot depend, in every instance, on the use of American combat troops. If genocide were to be the trigger for American military intervention, U.S. forces should have been dispatched to Cambodia, to northern Iraq, to southern Sudan, and to Burundi—all places where unspeakable horrors on a mass scale have been committed.

The war on genocide should be founded on a duty, a moral duty, to provide the victimized nation with the means of self-defense. The Afghan resistance prevailed over the Soviet intervention owing to American logistical help. Nations in imminent peril of genocidal attacks should receive no less. These are all measures that can be woven in with the judicious use of air power. The strug-

124   gle against genocide must be founded also on the notion of the *individual* responsibility of a guilty leadership; this responsibility can be translated into an unrelenting hounding of war criminals, both in office and in retirement. There are few reasons to condone the lavish circumstances enjoyed by the likes of Mengistu, Pol Pot, Amin, Duvalier, and Bokassa, to mention a few rulers with much blood on their hands. The war on genocide should, at a minimum, mean that those who commit genocide—and are formally indicted for the crime—shall never rest, that they shall enjoy neither immunity nor protection. They should have the legal status of outlaws, subject to seizure, just as pirates were for centuries. Their properties and financial assets should be frozen everywhere.

The issue of the proper relationship between diplomacy and force is raised in an acute fashion by the war in Bosnia and by the Vance-Owen plan. This war, like other ethnic conflicts, is a sanguinary and sordid affair. The Vance-Owen mission was criticized for continuing negotiations with Serb leaders tainted by war crimes, and for not insisting on the correction of repeated violations of the agreements they had concluded before continuing these negotiations.

Secretary of State Christopher's February 10, 1993, statement on the Balkans "makes clear" that the United States "is prepared to do its share to help implement and enforce an agreement that is acceptable to all sides."[2] The problem this pledge poses is what to do in the event of Serb violations. The plain military advantage of the Serb side and the record of the Serbs' behavior cast doubts that they will abide by any agreement. Much will depend on Russian positions. Should American servicemen be introduced in the Balkans—even if for peacekeeping purposes only—the issue of enforcement could become a grave matter. A war between American—or NATO—ground forces and the Serbs is bound to arouse dormant demons in Slavic lands. A war in the Balkans, to enforce an agreement based on the Vance-Owen plan, or for any other purpose, would invigorate isolationist passions in the United States; it might turn out to be the last foray of the United States in pursuit of world order concerns.

Christopher's statement unleashed a barrage of criticism for implicitly contemplating the entry of American ground forces in a part of the world from which there is no simple exit and in which they would be an easy target for a variety of hostile groups. The case for the deployment of American ground force, as part of a UN peacekeeping deployment in the Balkans, has not been made.

Neither has the case for American nonintervention been made. It is said that the circumstances that led to the First World War no longer prevail and that the Yugoslav crisis can be allowed to burn itself out without threatening the peace of the world. Indeed, the competition of the great powers in the Balkans is not a factor now; a local or even a regional war is unlikely to spread beyond the regional powers themselves. However, even from a coldly geopolitical perspective, there is cause for worry. A continuation of the war in the Balkans is fanning the flames of Islamic passions across a broad swath of countries; it is also feeding the revival of pan-Slavic sentiments in Russia and in the lands of Orthodoxy. This war has the power to precipitate atavistic hatreds that could lead to grave conflicts between the worlds once dominated by Islam and by the Eastern Church in Eurasia. It should be extinguished in haste.

126   The window for any kind of collective intervention under a Security Council umbrella could soon close, if threatened changes in Russian policies materialize. Russian nationalists and communists are joining hands to resist American leadership in the Balkans and elsewhere. The Yeltsin administration has already adopted a more assertive stand in the Baltics; in February 1993 the Russian parliament adopted, by an overwhelming vote (though with many members absent), a nonbinding resolution pressing for changes in Yeltsin's Balkans policy. It demanded that the Security Council impose sanctions on Croatia for its violations of the cease-fire or that it lift the sanctions on Serbia. The Clinton administration sought to enlist Russian support—and, indeed, participation—for any Balkan venture. The maintenance of a stable Russian-American relationship, which is central to world order, quite rightly remains an overriding concern. It is, however, a concern that should be shared equally on both sides.

★   ★   ★

The dissolution of Czechoslovakia and the establishment of the new European Economic Space on January 1, 1993, epitomize the turbulent forces that pull the nations of the world in opposing directions: toward wider union on one hand, and toward greater fragmentation on the other. It is as if the wheels of history were no longer synchronized, with their spokes grating and blocking rather than moving smoothly with the flow of time.

While economic imperatives and the power of the market dictate wider associations of states, the emotional and psychological drives to cultural and national affirmation support the currents of separation. The resulting forces that are pulling in three directions—wider associations of markets, narrower ethnic affirmation, and restrictive national sovereignty—continue to sap the stability of the post–Cold War world.

These are bad years for federations; the Soviet Union, Yugoslavia, and Czechoslovakia have all dissolved. Local and ethnic interests have prevailed over broader, state loyalties. The strains in Canada and the devolution pressures in Great Britain confirm that the problems of federation go beyond the adjustment of the states of eastern Europe to the collapse of communism. A deep undertow of national passions is sweeping the countries of East and West alike. Even in Switzerland, the paradigm of confederal success, some questioned the future of the country after the December 1992 vote—on ethnic lines—that rejected the European Economic Space.

Yet, paradoxically, federal solutions and confederal arrangements are proferred as the solution to the conflicts in Bosnia (Vance-Owen), in Cyprus ("set of ideas"), and between Israel and the Palestinians. Federal and confederal solutions are designed to deal with the issue of who shall govern so as to avoid the transfer of populations that often goes hand in hand with secession and separation. The federal approach is designed to assure that ethnic coexistence can prevail over ethnic separation and ethnic cleansing. To succeed, it must protect with credibility the rights of minorities and dispel the fears of atrocities that unleash streams of refugees. The paradox is that federalism is invoked as a remedy for situations that are far graver than those in the countries in which it has already failed.

In the final analysis, nothing can replace the decision, the will, to find political solutions to civil strife.

128   This political will does not often emerge without prodding from the outside and before hopes for military solutions have waned. The cultivation of a resolve to negotiate requires the wise application of political and economic pressures and inducements. It requires also a vision of the future that reconciles the claims of the sides, a vision that all sides can prefer over the struggle in which they are mired.

The exclusive position of the state, as the dominant actor in international relations in time of peace, is under challenge. The failure of the ideologies that saw in the state the principal instrument for lifting whole societies out of economic and social backwardness into the mainstream of international life has not dimmed the appeal of independence. Nor has the tragic and resounding failure of some of the states of Africa to assure the most basic essentials for the survival of their populations deterred the headlong rush of other nations to statehood. For many, a state continues to symbolize the hope of escape from the oppressive circumstances of the present; for small local elites, a state of their own offers shining personal prospects—the promise of status, of resources, and of positions, as well as an escape from provincial obscurity.

An ominous lesson to be drawn from the fate of the Kurds in Iraq and of the Muslims in Bosnia is that military power still counts in the life of small nations. In regional conflicts, regional balances of power, rather than promises of international assistance, determine the fate of local populations. The maintenance of regional peace requires a regional order based on local circumstances, rather than on the tenuous intervention of the international community. Collective intervention will no more guarantee the survival of "unimportant" peoples in the post–Cold War era than it did in earlier times. The lesson for these nations is stark: to survive, they must find ways of converting their survival into a matter of urgent concern for the great powers. This they can do either by a threatened extension of the conflicts in which they are at peril, or by gaining support—particularly in the United States—from their ethnic kin, or again by gaining access to weapons of mass destruction. The reluctance of the Western world to arm the Muslims in Bosnia is a portent for nations facing threats without the weapons to defend themselves; reliance on outside help is a weak reed indeed. The lesson for would-be Saddams or Milosevics is no less clear: to succeed, they must convince the powers that any military intervention will be costly in lives and in resources; that it would be difficult for the powers to extricate their forces; that their vital interests are not threatened by local ambitions; and that, moreover, military force will not restore the status quo ante. These are by no means new lessons, but they were overshadowed by expectations that a new order had dawned. They augur a fragmented world of heavily armed nations racing to acquire the terror weapons that are coming to world markets. The old order is fading fast; the very idea of "order," in the world that is taking shape before our eyes, is now in question.

Notes

INTRODUCTION

1. Patrick Daniel Moynihan published *Pandaemonium: Ethnicity in International Politics* (New York: Oxford Universtity Press, 1993) just as this book goes to press. His work ends with a call for fashioning responses to the ethnic and national conflicts that he analyses with great verve. "The challenge is to make the world safe for and from ethnicity, safe for just those differences which large assemblies, democratic or otherwise, will typically attempt to suppress. The idea deserves attention. As does the whole question of sovereignty."
2. E.H. Hobsbawm, *Nations and Nationalism Since 1780* (Cambridge: Cambridge University Press, second edition, 1992), p. 5.
3. Ibid., p. 9.
4. Moynihan, *Pandaemonium*, p. 125.
5. See the forceful discussion of ethnicity in the context of American multiculturalism in Arthur M. Schlesinger, *The Disuniting of America*, (New York: W.W. Norton, 1991.) The American scholar Donald L. Horowitz observed that "The study of ethnic conflict has often been a grudging concession to something distasteful, largely because, especially in the West, ethnic affiliations have been in disrepute." *Ethnic Groups in Conflict*, (Berkeley: University of California Press, 1985.)

   The essential work in this field is the erudite *The Ethnic Origins of Nations*, by Anthony D. Smith (Basil Blackwell, London, 1986) and its splendid bibliography. One of its principal concerns is the difference between ethnic communities and nations.

CHAPTER 1

1. On the Czechoslovak, Romanian, Greek, Yugoslav, and Iraqi treaties, see the useful discussion in C. A. Macartney, *National States and National Minorities* (New York: Russell & Russell, 1934). The study reviews the history and the operation of the minorities system in the

League of Nations. See also Georges Kaeckenbeeck, *The International Experiment of Upper Silesia* (Oxford: Oxford University Press, 1942), for an exhaustive and informative study of practice under a minority treaty.

2. The basic and essential feature of the state is that it is an organization endowed with the capacity to exert and control the use of force over certain people and within a given territory in the framework of a legal order that endows the state with authority. The American Law Institute defines a state as "an entity that has a defined territory and a permanent population, under the control of its own government, and that engages in, or has the capacity to engage in, formal relations with other such entities." See *Restatement of the Foreign Relations Law of the United States*, vol. 1, St. Paul, Minn.: American Law Institute, section 201. The most thorough treatment of this concept is in James Crawford, *The Creation of States in International Law* (Oxford: Clarendon Press, 1979).

CHAPTER 2

1. This position should not be confused with Francis Fukuyama's well-known thesis that liberal democracy is the triumphant ideology of the day. See his *The End of History and the Last Man* (New York: Free Press, 1992). The failure of statist ideologies of the left and the right does not signify the universal acceptance of the idea of liberal democracy.

2. 1951 Foreign Relations of the United States, vol. 1 (Washington, D.C.: GPO, 1951), p. 94.

3. Acheson is cited in Paul H. Nitze, Memorandum to Files, July 6, 1982. The memorandum is available to researchers in the Library of Congress.

4. Seventy-fifth American Assembly, *Rethinking America's Security* (New York: American Assembly, Columbia University, 1991).

5. For a brief and elegant summary of the history of the idea, see Alexandre Passerin d'Entreves, *The Notion of the State* (Oxford: Clarendon Press, 1967).

6. Robert Lansing, *Notes on Sovereignty* (Washington, D.C.: Carnegie Endowment, 1921), p. 15.

7. See George P. Shultz, "A Chance for Some Serious Diplomacy in the Middle East," *Washington Post*, March 6, 1990, p. 23.

8. An Assembly of European Regions was established in 1985. This was not an initiative of the members of the EC. It now has more than 200

members from both Eastern and Western Europe. It includes, for example, a majority of the English counties, most of Scotland's nine regions, artificial regions like Rhine-Westphalia, and the Moscow region. A region is defined as a level of government immediately below the central government with political representation guaranteed by the existence of an elected Regional Council, or failing this, by an association or body constituted at regional level by the local authorities at the level immediately below. Article 198 of the Maastricht Treaty contemplates the creation of a 24-member Committee of the Regions consisting of regional and local bodies from the Community only. The relationship between the Committee on Regions and the Assembly of European Regions remains to be determined. See *New Statesman and Society*, vol. 5, no. 207, June 19, 1992, pp. 16–28.

9. Document of the Copenhagen Meeting of the Conference of the Human Dimension of the CSCE, June 1990, reprinted in *International Legal Materials*, vol. 29 (September, 1990), p. 1305.

10. Fukuyama, *The End of History*, p. 42.

11. Seventy-fifth American Assembly, *Rethinking America's Security*, p. 21.

12. Michael W. Doyle, "Kant, Liberal Legacies and Foreign Affairs," *Philosophy and Public Affairs*, vol. 12 (Summer 1983), p. 205.

13. Jacob L. Talmon, *The Origins of Totalitarian Democracy* (London: Secker and Warburg, 1952).

14. Isaiah Berlin, "The Bent Twig: A Note on Nationalism," *Foreign Affairs*, vol. 51 (October 1972), p. 11.

15. See Morton H. Halperin and David J. Scheffer with Patricia L. Small, *Self-Determination in the New World Order* (Washington, D.C.: Carnegie Endowment for International Peace, 1992).

16. Ibid., p. 80.

17. General Assembly resolution 2625 (October, 1970).

18. See his speech at Princeton University delivered on December 12, 1991, reprinted in *U.S. Department of State Dispatch*, vol. 2 (1991), p. 890.

19. European Community, "Declaration on the Guidelines on the European Community Recognition of New States in Eastern Europe and in the Soviet Union," EPC Press Release 128/91, December 16, 1992.

20. This was a system of protection developed in a series of treaties concluded after the First World War for the benefit of national, religious, and ethnic minorities in a belt of states that stretched from the Baltic to the Aegean, to the Black Sea, and further east to the confines of Persia. It provided for a system of League of Nations guarantees that "at the best . . . has acted as a local anaesthetic against certain cases of preventible suffering; it has not operated as a cure for the disease." See

C. A. Macartney, *National States and National Minorities* (New York:
Russell & Russell, 1934), p. 420.

21. See Jay A. Sigler, *Minority Rights* (Westport, Conn.: Greenwood Press, 1983), ch. 4.

22. Macartney characterizes the responses of the states subjected to the League procedure in these words: "We [the governments] might be able to put up with this if all states were liable, in their turn, to appear in the same box, but they are not. Why should this discrimination be shewn against us? Do we, Poland, treat our minorities worse than Italy, or than Germany treated her Polish subjects before the war— Germany who hates us, who uses these treaties to besmirch our name and stir up disaffection within our borders. . . . are we, Czechoslovakia, a less civilized nation than Bolivia or Uruguay? This . . . is a fair statement of the Treaty states' complaints." See Macartney, *National States*, p. 372.

23. For a thoughtful discussion of the problem of minorities in the aftermath of the Second World War, see Inis L. Claude, *National Minorities—An International Problem* (Cambridge, Mass.: Harvard University Press, 1955). For a recent consideration of the issue, see the comprehensive work of Hurst Hannum, *Autonomy, Sovereignty and Self-Determination* (Philadelphia: University of Pennsylvania Press, 1990); see also the stimulating work of Robert H. Jackson, *Quasi-States: Sovereignty, International Relations and the Third World* (Cambridge University Press, 1990). For a useful text on autonomy regimes, see Yoram Dinstein, *Models of Autonomy* (New Brunswick, N.J.: Transaction Press, 1981).

24. Draft Union treaty, FBIS-SOV-91-124, June 27, 1991 p. 26.

25. See Gidon Gottlieb, "From Autonomy to a Framework State," in T. Buergenthal, ed., *Issues in Contemporary International Law: Essays in Honor of Professor Louis B. Sohn* (Arlington, V.A.: N.P. Engel, 1984).

26. This is a reference to the tradition of state centralism named for the Jacobin faction in the French National Assembly during the Revolution of 1789.

27. See Lea Brilmayer, "Secession and Self-Determination: A Territorial Interpretation," *Yale Journal of International Law*, vol. 16 (1991), p. 177. Brilmayer argues that the issue in self-determination disputes is not between peoples and states, but between people, states, and territory.

28. See chapter 1, note 2, on the term "state." The UN General Assembly resolutions regarding the right of self-determination and the covenants for the protection of human rights refer to "peoples."

29. States use these concepts in different ways. Those with an assimilationist tradition grant the state's "nationality" to individuals. Thus, once a person is naturalized, that person is said to have ceased to belong

134   to any other national group. On the other hand, states with a pluralistic tradition recognize the separate national existence of different groups within their borders. In such states, the acquisition of the citizenship of the state does not dissolve the bond of nationality. The concepts of nationality and of citizenship bear different meanings in states with different traditions. The usage of these terms is therefore fraught with considerable ambiguity.

CHAPTER 3

1. The issue of ripeness is a separate one. It is ably considered in Richard Haass, *Conflicts Unending* (New Haven: Yale University Press, 1989).
2. "Review and Outlook: Turkey's Overload," *Wall Street Journal* (European Edition) November 29, 1992, p. 8.
3. The relationship with Teheran is not without its problems. Prime Minister Suleyman Demirel of Turkey said he did not rule out Iranian involvement in political murders committed in his country.
4. Monteagle Stearns, *Entangled Allies* (New York: Council on Foreign Relations, 1992), p. 124.
5. See *Report of the Secretary General on his Mission of Good Offices in Cyprus,* S/24472, August 21, 1992.
6. See *Report of the Secretary General of the United Nations on his Mission of Good Offices in Cyprus* in regard to the resumed joint meetings in October and November 1992, S/24830, November 19, 1992. See also Security Council resolution 789 (November 25, 1992), which chides the Turkish Cypriot side for taking positions that are not consistent with the set of ideas.
7. *Report of the UN Secretary General*, November 19, 1992, S/24830, p. 11.
8. See Judy Dempsey, "UN Paves the Way for Troops in Sarajevo," in *Financial Times*, June 11, 1992, p. 14.
9. George P. Shultz, "Bosnia: Transcript of Informal Remarks," International Rescue Committee, December 7, 1992.
10. See the Declaration on the Rights of Persons Belonging to National or Ethnic, Religious and Linguistic Minorities adopted by the U.N. General Assembly at its Forty-seventh session, resolution 47/135.
11. See *Report of the Secretary General on the Activities of the International Conference on the former Yugoslavia*, January 6, 1993, S/25050.
12. Rebecca West, *Black Lamb and Grey Falcon* (New York: Penguin Books,) p. 618.

CHAPTER 4

1. Resolution 46/182 (December 19, 1991).
2. Louis Henkin, "The Use of Force: Law and U.S. Policy," in L. Henkin et al., *Right v. Might* (New York: Council on Foreign Relations, 1989), p. 61.
3. Thomas Franck, "Agora: the Powers of Appreciation: Who Is the Ultimate Guardian of UN Legality?" *American Journal of International Law*, vol. 86 (July 1992), p. 519.
4. Henry Kissinger, "False Dreams of a New World Order," *Washington Post*, February 26, 1991.
5. As quoted by Henry Kissinger, "False Dreams of a New World Order," *Washington Post*, February 26, 1991, p. 21.
6. Charles Krauthammer, "The Lonely Superpower," *New Republic*, July 21, 1991, p. 23.
7. The only exception, and a theoretical one at that, is to be found in the United Nations Participation Act. This statute opens a hypothetical path for the use of force without the approval of Congress. It authorizes the use of force by the United States without such approval upon a decision of the Security Council. But the provisions of the act that permit the use of force without congressional authority are not in effect. They would become operative only when the agreements contemplated under article 43 of the Charter are concluded and ratified; and their ratification would, of course, require further Senate approval.
8. Gorbachev revealed that he had urged the president not to intervene unilaterally; we do not know how much weight this request carried.
9. It is no less telling that the administration made no reference either to collective security or to the UN when it decided to launch Operation Just Cause to dislodge Panamanian leader Manuel Noriega. The administration was willing not only to ignore the Security Council, but also to use force in apparent violation of its international obligations.
10. Article 51 provides: "Nothing in the present Charter shall impair the inherent right of individual or collective self defense if an armed attack occurs against a Member of the United Nations, until the Security Council has taken the measures necessary to maintain international peace and security."
11. Eugene Rostow, "Until What? Enforcement Action or Collective Self-Defense?" *American Journal of International Law*, vol. 85 (July, 1991), p. 511.
12. Article 53 of the Charter provides: "The Security Council shall, where appropriate, utilize such regional arrangements or agencies for enforcement action under its authority. But no enforcement action shall be

taken under regional arrangements or by regional agencies without the authorization of the Security Council."

13. Boutros Boutros-Ghali, *An Agenda for Peace* (New York: United Nations, 1992), p. 18.

14. See David Hendrickson, "Toward a Practical Vision of Collective Action for International Peace and Security" (Paper for a Round Table on Defining a New World Order, Fletcher School of Law and Diplomacy, May 2–3, 1991). See also Brian Urquhart, "Who Can Stop Civil Wars?" *New York Times*, December 29, 1991.

15. In the case of Iraq, as part of the sanctions regime, the Security Council decreed a levy on the shipment of Iraqi oil in international commerce. It thus, almost unnoticed, established the principle of a fiscal base of its own outside the framework of the UN's regular budgetary procedures.

16. Address to West Point cadets, "Bush's Talk to Cadets: When Force Makes Sense," *New York Times* January 6, 1993, p. 6.

CHAPTER 5

1. It may be useful here to restate the policy dilemma involving national and ethnic minorities as it was perceived in the years before the Second World War: "Where fate has placed a nationally conscious minority in a state there are only three possible solutions, and (although few governments believe this) forcible denationalization is not one of them. Perhaps a fourth should be counted—physical slaughter; but although this most effective of all remedies is still in vogue in certain countries it shall not be discussed in this humane essay. The three possibilities which are to be considered are these: either the theoretical basis and existing populations may be left untouched, but the frontiers may be revised in such a way as to leave alien elements outside them; or the basis of the state may be retained, and its frontiers left intact, but the minorities may be eliminated by emigration (perhaps through exchange of populations); or thirdly, existing populations and frontiers may be retained, but the basis of the state may be altered." See C. A. Macartney, *National States and National Minorities* (New York: Russell & Russell, 1934), pp. 422–423.

2. For the text of his remarks, see "Christopher's Remarks on Balkans: 'Crucial Test,' " *New York Times*, February 11, 1993, p. 6.

Bibliographical Note on Nationalism and Ethnicity

For a useful introductory text on the classical literature see A. Passerin d'Entreves, *The Notion of the
State* (Oxford, 1967). He makes the point that
the idea of nation is entirely absent from the definition of
the state which can be found in the writings of the
thinkers—Machiavelli, Bodin and Hobbes—who first
mapped out the new landscape of the modern political
world. " . . . [T]here would seem to have been from
the beginning two possible ways of conceiving the nation: one based on purely 'natural' factors, the other on
'spiritual' elements; the one on something given, the
other on something desired. The first of these two con-
ceptions may have begun by merely stressing linguistic
and ethnical differentiation as the distinguishing factors
of nationality. It ended by extolling the most dubious
biological factors, blood and race. The second concep-
tion, on the contrary, was based on the recognition of
the importance of the cultural bond." (p. 179)

The linguistic criterion of nationhood is considered
at some length in Anthony D. Smith, *Nationalism, Theories of Nationalism* (New York: Harper & Row, second
edition, 1983), which contains an excellent bibliography. The linguistic aspects of nationalism are also dis-

138   cussed in the brilliant book of E.J. Hobsbawm, *Nations and Nationalism Since 1780* (Cambridge: Cambridge University Press, second edition, 1992.) The war between Bosnian Serbs and Muslims, who speak the same language, is a striking reminder that language and nationalism cannot be equated.

For another excellent bibliography see Anthony D. Smith's more recent book, *The Ethnic Origins of Nations* (Oxford: Oxford University Press, England, 1986).

Other important recent works include:

Benedict Anderson, *Imagined Communities: Reflections on the Origins and Spread of Nationalism*, (London: Verso, rev. ed., 1991)

J. Breuilly, *Nationalism and the State*, (Manchester: Manchester University Press, 1982).

Helene Carrere d'Encausse, *Decline of an Empire: The Soviet Socialist Republic in Revolt*, (New York: Newsday Books, 1979).

Walker Connor, *The National Question in Marxist-Leninist Theory and Strategy* (Princeton: Princeton University Press, 1984).

Ernest Gellner, *Nations and Nationalism*, (Ithaca, N.Y.: Cornell University Press, 1983).

Milton M. Gordon, *Assimilation in American Life: The Role of Race, Religion and National Origin*, (New York: Oxford University Press, 1964).

F. H. Hinsley, *Nationalism and the International System*, (London: Hodder and Stoughton, 1973).

Donald L. Horowitz, *Ethnic Groups in Conflict* (Berkeley: University of California Press, 1985).

Harold Isaacs, *Idols of the Tribe: Group Identity and Political Change* (New York: Harper and Row, 1975).

Daniel P. Moynihan, *Pandaemonmium, Ethnicity in Inter-* 139
national Politics (Oxford: Oxford University Press,
1993.)

Richard Pipes, *The Formation of the Soviet Union: Com-*
munism and Nationalism, 1917–1923 (Cambridge,
Mass.: Harvard University Press, 1949).

A. Zolberg and M. Esman, eds., *Ethnic Conflict in the*
Western World (Ithaca, N.Y.: Cornell University
Press, 1977).

See also Isaiah Berlin, "Two Concepts of Nationalism:
An Interview with Isaiah Berlin," *The New York Review*
of Books, November 21, 1991, p. 22.

INDEX